ELEVATE OTHERS

LESSONS *for* PURPOSE-DRIVEN ENTREPRENEURS

DAVID TRENT

ELEVATE OTHERS

LESSONS *for* PURPOSE-DRIVEN
ENTREPRENEURS

DAVID TRENT

"David Trent offers a fresh, transformative approach to success. Through personal stories and powerful insights, Trent reveals how elevating others is the key to thriving in business and life. Entrepreneurs will discover the power of resilience, mentorship, and the unique philosophy of "altruistic egoism," where helping others unlocks your own potential. Packed with actionable wisdom from Trent's 36-year journey, this book will inspire you to build deeper relationships, lead with purpose, and achieve true fulfillment. If you're ready to redefine success, this is a must-read."

Jerome Myers, Founder, CEO, and Author of *Your NEXT*

"Two things struck me powerfully about this book. First, don't reinvent the wheel. Reinvention is less important - and less valuable for an entrepreneur than optimization. Take a good idea and make it great! Second, I love how the author honors commitment. I've always believed that what separates an entrepreneur from the rest of the pack if that he/she/they will do what 95% of others won't. That's the difference - and it's not nothing."

Mike Malatesta, CEO, and Author of *Owner Shift*

"David Trent's message resonated deeply with me. Chapters 7, "Clues," and 8, "Commit," stood out for their practical insights. Trent emphasizes the importance of learning from mentors instead of reinventing the wheel, highlighting that many quit just before achieving success. He advocates for surrounding ourselves with positive influences and maintaining commitment to our goals. This genuine approach to success is refreshing and applicable, making his book a valuable resource for anyone looking to navigate their entrepreneurial journey."

Paul Peters: Founder, CEO, and Author of *The Ways of Wisdom*

"David Trent has created a handbook for inspiring current and future entrepreneurs to live their purpose through their companies. With a clear theme for each chapter broken into stories that resonate with that same theme, David's clear, concise writing and vulnerability in sharing his failures and successes as an entrepreneur are inspiring. I highly recommend *Elevate Others*, especially for new grads, be it high school or university."

Hamish Knox, CEO, and Author of *Accountability the Sandler Way*

"Get ready to be captivated by this unique book! In a world overflowing with "how-to" guides, David Trent offers something refreshingly different. He masterfully blends the principles of success in life and business with compelling stories from his personal journey and the inspiring people he's met along the way. "Focus on elevating others, and you'll unlock the secret to true business success." Having witnessed David live this philosophy firsthand, I'm excited that we can now all benefit from these powerful lessons and insights."

Darrell Amy, Founder and Author of *Revenue Growth Engine*

DISCLAIMER

This book is designed to provide competent, reliable, and educational information regarding business growth and other subject matter covered. However, it is sold with the understanding the author and publisher specifically disclaim all responsibility for any liability, loss, or risk, personal or otherwise, incurred as a consequence, directly or indirectly, of the use and application of any of the contents of this publication.

In order to maintain the anonymity of others, the names and identifying characteristics of some people, places, and organizations described in this book have been changed.

The opinions, ideas, and recommendations contained in this publication do not necessarily represent those of the Publisher. The use of any information provided in this book is solely at your own risk.

Know that the author shared their tools, practices, and knowledge with you with a sincere and generous intent to assist you on your business journey. Please contact them with any questions you may have about the techniques or information they provided. They will be happy to assist you further and be an ongoing resource for your success!

RECEIVE EXCLUSIVE CONTENT AND MORE!

Visit https://trentpremiergrowth.com/elevate-others-bonus-content/

or scan

to receive your free digital copy of **The Gear 10 Formula**

and delve deeper with David Trent.

Don't miss out on future updates and insider access—

join our community today!

*To my incredible wife, Tiny, whose unwavering support
and encouragement have been a guiding light throughout this journey.
Your willingness to read every chapter as soon as I finished,
along with your constructive criticism and thoughtful guidance,
has been invaluable. This being my first book, your insights have
made the process not only enjoyable but also a true blessing.
As you often remind me, "David, your words have the power
to inspire others," and that sentiment has fueled
my passion to share this message.*

*I also dedicate this book to the countless individuals
who have shaped my journey—my family, friends, mentors,
and clients. Your encouragement has been the foundation
of my success. A heartfelt thank you to all the test readers who
generously offered their time and feedback; your insights allowed
me to make significant improvements and refine my message.*

TABLE OF CONTENTS

ESTABLISHING SUCCESS | 95

MY 40s AND 50s AT TRENT CAPITAL MANAGEMENT–
INNOVATING AND INVESTING IN OTHERS

REFLECTION ON THE LEGACY | 142

MY LATE 50s AND LATER YEARS AT TRENT CAPITAL MANAGEMENT–
EMBRACING WISDOM AND PERSPECTIVE

INTRODUCTION

Welcome to *ELEVATE OTHERS, Lessons for Purpose-Driven Entrepreneurs.*

After a 36-year odyssey in entrepreneurship and starting, building, and successfully exiting my first company, Trent Capital Management, I can tell you that it's the people who made the difference in my life and business, who truly created my success.

Make it your focus to elevate others and you have the secret to authentic business success.

Whether you're a visionary entrepreneur, a resolute business leader, a nurturing parent, or an individual on a quest for personal growth, the wisdom and mindset training here will help you be in it for the good of others, which will transform and shape your business and life into the vision you started so passionately with.

In the vast landscape of entrepreneurship, where dreams collide with challenges and ambitions weave intricate paths, one concept stands out like a beacon of light: Be in it for the good of others! Join me and explore the impact this will have on your journey and business.

At 60 years old, I'm reflecting on a career that began at 24, driven by passion, determination, and an unyielding pursuit of growth. I founded Trent Capital Management from scratch at age 33 in 1996. Fast forward to the fall of 2020. My company grew to serve over 200 families with $200 million in assets under management (AUM), generating $2.2 million in revenue and $1.1 million in profits, with a company enterprise value north of $6 million. In January 2021, I merged with two partners at Legacy Capital, becoming a 40% owner in that enterprise.

By September 30, 2023, we served over 500 families and managed a combined $1.1 billion in assets. At this point, I sold my interest and fully exited.

Breaking the billion-dollar barrier in assets under management is no small feat—it's a summit reached by only 7% of Registered Investment Advisory firms in the US. For me, hitting this rarified air felt like conquering Mount Everest after years of relentless climbing. Each dollar represented countless hours of hard work and client trust. As I stood at this pinnacle of success, I realized it was the perfect moment to bow out gracefully. What better high note to exit on than achieving something so extraordinary in our industry?

Along the journey, I also started another company called Absolute Athlete and bought another from a client. Though smaller, these ventures testify to the entrepreneurial spirit that burns within me. Today, in early July 2024, despite being financially independent, my love for entrepreneurship and relationships has led me to create and invest in three new ventures: Trent Premier Growth, Optima M&A, and Absolute Capital, all outside my former focus in wealth management.

Amidst the numbers and milestones, it's the people who left an indelible mark on my journey. My experience taught me that I'm happiest when cultivating current relationships and establishing new ones. Why? I came across a phrase in a book called *Halftime:* "Altruistic egoism." It's an irony when you feed your ego by how you help, love, and support others.

This concept highlights a beautiful synergy between self-interest and selflessness. By deriving satisfaction from helping others, we create a virtuous cycle that benefits both the giver and the receiver. It's a powerful realization that our own well-being can be intrinsically linked to the welfare of those around us.

A great example is my good friend Marlon Haynes, who, in the presence of other friends, recently gushed about how much I impacted his mindset and thus his results in both business and personal life. "David, you've completely shifted how I approach life, business, and challenges.

Your encouragement and wisdom have been a game-changer for me," he said with genuine enthusiasm. His words were a powerful reminder of the profound joy and fulfillment that comes from meaningful connections and selfless service. It was moments like these that reinforced my belief in the importance of uplifting others and the lasting impact we can have on each other's lives.

The **ELEVATE OTHERS** concept grew naturally from my upbringing and life experiences. My parents were deeply invested in my siblings and me, always focusing on our character development and what was best for us. They taught us about the importance of service through their work in building a family-owned insurance agency, as well as their active involvement in church and community leadership. Guided by the ultimate example of service, Jesus Christ, they showed us the profound impact of being committed to the well-being of others. It's an example I still remember in everything I do today.

My mother always emphasized the importance of our Christian faith. One indelible example of this was her dedication to teaching and guiding Sunday school classes for various ages throughout my childhood and into adulthood. She loved this role, knowing she was making a difference in others' lives. I don't think she fully grasped what a phenomenal example she set for me and my siblings. "Every time you help someone or show kindness," she'd say with a warm smile, "you're letting God's light shine through you."

My brother Keith, who was four years older than me, seemed like a natural leader, but his leadership skills developed through my parents' example and teachings. Keith was a super achiever.

Out of a class of over 400 students in high school, he was valedictorian, All-State in football, and student body president. On top of that, he preached a sermon one Sunday in our church. My family was a huge influence, but so were books!

While I wasn't an avid reader in my youth, that changed in my 20s. As I mapped out my path and worked out what I wanted to be, I dedicated significant time to reading. A couple of my all-time favorites are *The Art of*

Exceptional Living by Jim Rohn and *See You at the Top* by Zig Ziglar. I have two favorite quotes from these philosophers.

Jim Rohn's famous quote about the greatest value in life is: "The major reason for setting a goal is for what it makes of you to accomplish it." This quote emphasizes that the true value lies in personal growth and self-improvement rather than the external rewards.

Zig Ziglar's famous quote states: "If you help enough other people get what they want, you'll get what you want." The essence of this quote is that by focusing on helping and serving others, rather than just pursuing your own goals, you will ultimately achieve greater success and fulfillment.

I also listened to audio cassettes from great teachers and philosophers, with Earl Nightingale and Jim Rohn being among my favorites. I consumed a lot of those old audio cassette programs back in the day.

A couple (of many) nuggets from those tapes that I teach today:

Jim Rohn's electrifying words echo through the ages: "Let others leave their future in someone else's hands, but not you!" This battle cry underscores the vital importance of taking the reins of your own destiny and refusing to be a mere passenger on the journey of life.

Earl Nightingale offers a quote that unlocks the secrets of the universe: "Whatever we plant in our subconscious mind and nourish with repetition and emotion will one day become a reality." This is the key to manifesting our dreams and aspirations. With dedicated focus and passion, we can train our subconscious to bring forth the life we desire.

As I journaled throughout my life, a clear pattern emerged—one of lessons learned, wisdom gained, and insights shared.

This book is structured based on those patterns into short chapters, each offering a bite-sized lesson categorized into three sections: Entrepreneurial Inspiration, Family Values, and Master Teachings. The book's chronology is woven through my entrepreneurial journey, which began when I was 24. This structure highlights pivotal moments and valuable teachings from my family and mentors in a practical way you can apply quickly and effectively for your own journey.

The Entrepreneurial Inspiration stories are a tapestry of experiences, successes, failures, and breakthroughs. They highlight the resilience, adaptability, and relentless pursuit of excellence that define the entrepreneurial spirit.

The Family Values delve into the fabric of my upbringing, the values instilled by my parents and grandparents, and the lessons learned from family dynamics. These tales are not just about business; they're about life, love, relationships, and the importance of staying grounded amidst success.

The Master Teachings section pays homage to the authors, mentors, and thought leaders whose words shaped my mindset, influenced my decisions, and guided me through challenges. From books, podcasts, and other sources, these teachers imparted wisdom that transcended business and touched the core of personal growth and fulfillment.

Twenty-five compact volumes brimming with 2000+ words of wisdom await you here. Enjoy each simple title and theme, such as Start, Duty, Prayer, Mornings, Words, and Challenges, that offer you seamless navigation and the opportunity to delve into the lessons that resonate most deeply with your journey.

My hope is that this book becomes a lifelong companion and source of inspiration, guidance, and motivation. May it empower you to embrace the *ELEVATE OTHERS* mindset—to be in for the good of others—and create a lasting impact, much like the impact I had on my friend Marlon. Embrace this growing and evolving mindset in your journey of entrepreneurship and life.

THE FORMATIVE YEARS

MY 20s AT NEW YORK LIFE –
BUILDING RESILIENCE
AND CONFIDENCE

"You don't have to be great to start,
but you have to start to be great."

~ Zig Ziglar

CHAPTER ONE

START

ENTREPRENEURIAL INSPIRATION
How a Humble Start at Twin City Bank
Ignited My Entrepreneurial Spirit

As a recent college graduate in the early months of 1986, I faced the harsh reality of a challenging job market. The prospect of landing a job seemed daunting and almost unattainable. I remember sitting at my small desk in my cramped apartment, staring at the classifieds section of the newspaper.

Is this all there is? Will I ever find a job that's right for me?

It was a challenging time, but when I finally landed a role as a management trainee at Twin City Bank, it was like winning the lottery. Although banking wasn't my true passion, it was the only option available at the time, and I was grateful for the opportunity.

"You did it, David!" my mom exclaimed when I told her the news. "This is your foot in the door. Who knows where it might lead?"

Her words echoed in my mind as I walked into Twin City Bank on my first day, a mix of excitement and nervousness coursing through me.

Little did I know that this job would become the foundation of my career and shape my aspirations.

Working at Twin City Bank provided me with a valuable platform to gain experience and insights into the world of finance. And the best part? The camaraderie among my colleagues created a supportive environment that fueled both my personal and professional growth.

"Hey, David, want to grab lunch?" my colleague Tom would often ask. These lunch breaks became impromptu mentoring sessions, where I soaked up knowledge like a sponge.

However, amidst the friendly atmosphere and learning opportunities, I couldn't ignore certain discrepancies. The salary was a mere $15,000, and the prospect of increasing that income seemed like a distant and arduous journey. It made me question my long-term goals and financial ambitions.

One night, as I pored over my monthly budget, trying to make ends meet, a thought struck me.

Is this all I'm worth? There has to be more to life than just scraping by.

This realization led me to a moonlighting opportunity in life insurance sales.

Later in life, a particular quote from Zig Ziglar became a part of me, resonating deeply even now: "You don't have to be great to start, but you have to start to be great."

I now realize my decision to explore life insurance on the side perfectly embodied that quote. I yearned to boost my earnings and delve into entrepreneurship, so I took the leap and **started** venturing into this new territory.

With the guidance of a friend of my dad's, Bob Hamilton, an experienced life insurance agent, and the assistance of my father's insurance files, I took my first steps into the world of entrepreneurship. Bob and I met in the evenings at my father's office, making phone calls and searching for potential prospects for life insurance sales.

"Remember, David," Bob would say, his voice filled with enthusiasm, "every no gets you closer to a yes. Don't let rejection discourage you."

I'd nod, take a deep breath, and dial the next number, my heart racing with each ring. "Hello, Mrs. Johnson? This is David Trent. I'm calling to discuss how life insurance can protect your family's future. . ."

Although my initial venture into entrepreneurship didn't bring exceptional success, it was a valuable learning experience. It ignited my passion for exploring new territories and paved the way for future endeavors.

After spending over a year at Twin City Bank, I found myself at a crossroads. The security of my banking job felt like a safety net, but the allure of entrepreneurship was calling. I remember standing in front of the mirror one morning, adjusting my tie, when I caught my own gaze.

Is this really what you want, David? Are you content with playing it safe, or are you ready to take a risk for something greater?

That moment of self-reflection led me to make the bold decision to transition into the insurance industry full time. This led me to New York Life in the fall of 1987, where I embraced a commission-based role and laid the foundation for my entrepreneurial journey.

As I walked into the New York Life office on my first day, a mix of excitement and trepidation filled me.

This is it, No more safety net. It's all on me now.

And with that thought, I took my first step into the world of true entrepreneurship, ready to face whatever lay ahead.

FAMILY VALUES

From Shoe Factory to Reliable Life: The Inspiring Story of My Parents' Resilience and Determination

In 1954, fresh out of high school, Mom and Dad, newly married, embarked on a bold journey as they stepped into the workforce at the shoe factory. Their dedication and hard work were evident as they poured their time and effort into their jobs, each earning a modest wage ranging from 75 cents to $1.00 per hour. This marked the beginning of their shared path towards financial stability and building a life together.

Their journey took a significant turn on January 22, 1956, with the arrival of their first bundle of joy, my sister, Terry. It was then that Mom faced a tough decision, choosing to leave her job at the shoe factory to prioritize raising their child. With only one income of $40 per week, their financial situation became more challenging, yet their determination to provide for their growing family remained steadfast.

Dad's friend George Barnett shared insights about his life insurance career, where he found success and fulfillment. I remember Dad talking about George and how he shared insights about the life insurance "debit" industry. "George would tell us about all the success he experienced, and I got so excited I called in sick one day so I could travel to Little Rock," said Dad.

This decision marked a pivotal moment in Dad's career journey. Dad interviewed and was hired by Reliable Life.

On his first Monday, his boss called him aside and said, "You're taking the insurance exam on Thursday." This worried him, as he wasn't a great student and had no insurance knowledge. "Don't worry, you'll be fine," his boss assured him, "Don't fret!"

The exam only had 25 questions, and a helpful person from the insurance department assisted him with the answers. "The insurance commissioner got a turkey from Reliable Life every Christmas," Dad told me with a chuckle. Dad passed the exam and started his insurance career on April 7, 1958, earning $75 per week!

Dad's journey in the insurance industry wasn't without hurdles. Assigned to impoverished communities in Little Rock, North Little Rock, and Benton, Arkansas, Dad was challenged going door-to-door collecting small sums (sometimes as little as ten cents per week) from customers. Despite his initial nervousness and trembling hands, Dad's determination to succeed and provide for his family fueled his perseverance.

"I remember my manager coming with me the first week and telling me that I was probably not cut out for this job because of my shyness and nervousness," Dad recalled, his voice filled with indignation. "That really angered me and made me even more determined to prove him wrong."

"I remember feeling nervous, and my hands would tremble as I approached each house," Dad continued. "I had never done anything like this before, and it was intimidating to ask people for money, even if it was just a few cents."

Despite his initial hesitation, Dad's determination to succeed and provide for his family kept him going. "I knew that this job was important for our future, and I couldn't let my fear, or anyone's doubts hold me back," he said. "Every time I collected a payment, no matter how small, it was a step closer to achieving my goals."

As Dad gained experience and confidence, he became more comfortable in his role. He developed relationships with his customers and learned to empathize with their struggles. "Many of the people I visited were living in poverty, but they always found a way to pay their premiums," he said. "It was humbling to see their toughness and commitment to protecting their families."

Dad's perseverance and dedication paid off as he climbed the ranks in the insurance industry. Mom and Dad's story embodies the essence of that Zig Ziglar quote, "You don't have to be great to start, but you have to start to be great." Their courage to embark on new paths, face obstacles head-on and make bold decisions laid the foundation for their successful careers and the life they built together.

As I think back on their journey, I often ask, *Would I have had the same courage? Could I have faced those challenges with the same resilience?* Their story isn't just an inspiration but a guiding light on my own entrepreneurial journey.

MASTER TEACHINGS
Breaking Free from Self-Imposed Limits: The Power of Zig Ziglar's Flea Training

I'll never forget the first time I heard Zig Ziglar speak about his flea training analogy. I was at a seminar, feeling stuck in my career and unsure of how to move forward. As Zig took the stage, his energy was infectious, and I leaned forward, eager to absorb every word.

"Folks, let me tell you about fleas," Zig began, his Southern drawl filling the room. "You see, it's all about learning to train fleas."

I remember thinking, *Fleas? What on Earth does this have to do with success?* But as Zig continued, I felt a shift in perspective.

"Imagine putting fleas in a Mason jar and sealing the lid shut," Zig said, gesturing with his hands. "Naturally, the fleas will start jumping, as that's what fleas love to do. However, as they continue jumping, they'll inevitably bump their heads on the jar's lid."

I could almost see those fleas jumping in my mind, and I started to draw parallels to my own life. *How many times have I hit my own metaphorical lid?*

Zig's voice grew more animated as he continued, "At first, they'll keep trying to reach their full potential, but after a while, something interesting happens."

He paused for effect, and I held my breath, waiting for the revelation.

"The fleas adjust their behavior," Zig explained, his eyes twinkling. "They no longer jump high enough to hit the lid. They've conditioned themselves to jump just below the lid's height."

I felt a pang of recognition. *Wasn't that exactly what I had been doing in my career? Playing it safe, staying within my comfort zone?*

"And here's the kicker," Zig said, shaking his head, "even when you remove the lid, the fleas remain confined within their limits. They've mentally restricted themselves to a certain height, unable to explore the vast space beyond."

As those words sank in, I felt a mix of emotions wash over me. Disappointment in myself for setting my own limits, but also a spark of hope.

If I can recognize these self-imposed boundaries, can't I also break free from them?

Zig's voice rose with conviction as he drove his point home. "You've got to be willing to start," he declared. "Refuse to settle for mediocrity. Embrace resilience, determination, and a growth mindset. That's how you soar higher and achieve the extraordinary in your personal and professional endeavors."

I found myself nodding along, my mind racing with possibilities. *What if I stopped hitting my head against imaginary lids? What if I dared to jump higher than ever before?*

As I left the seminar that day, I couldn't shake Zig's words from my mind. *Am I really living up to my full potential? Or have I been training myself to stay small, like those fleas in the jar?*

That night, I sat down and made a list of all the "lids" I had placed on myself—the self-doubt, fear of failure, and the comfort of the familiar. And then, inspired by Zig's teaching, I made another list of all the ways I could start breaking through those limitations.

From that day forward, whenever I felt myself hesitating or holding back, I heard Zig's voice in my head: "You've got to be willing to start." It became my mantra, pushing me to take risks, reach higher, and refuse to settle for less than my best.

Zig Ziglar's flea training analogy didn't just teach me about success it showed me how to recognize and overcome the mental barriers that held me back. It was a turning point in my journey, one that set me on a path to achieving things I never thought possible.

TRENT TAKEAWAYS

- START—greatness is a pursuit.

- Grow into your goals.

- What doors can you "unlock" in pursuit of bigger dreams?

"Failure is the condiment that gives success its flavor."

~Truman Capote

CHAPTER 2

SELL

ENTREPRENEURIAL INSPIRATION

From Novice to Veteran:
A 36-Year Journey of Persistence, Adaptation, and Growth in the Unforgiving World of Sales

In the fall of 1987, at the ripe age of 24, I set off on a remarkable adventure that left an indelible mark on my professional path: the world of sales. Taking the plunge as a W-2 employee at New York Life, where my income relied solely on commissions, felt like diving headfirst into the thrilling realm of entrepreneurship.

As I sat in my tiny cubicle on my first day:

What have I gotten myself into? Can I really make a living just by talking to people?

The excitement of the unknown battled with my self-doubt. Sales, however, proved to be a formidable challenge. The odds were stacked against me, especially at such a young age, but I was determined to crack the code of success. My inexperience loomed large, and the complexities of the insurance industry seemed overwhelming.

During a particularly tough week, I remember staring at my phone, willing it to ring. "Come on, David," I muttered to myself. "You can do this. Just pick up the phone and make the call." My hand hovered over the receiver, trembling slightly. The fear of rejection was paralyzing.

I constantly second-guessed my decisions, wondering if I truly understood the products I was selling or if I could effectively communicate their value to potential clients. The fear of rejection and the pressure to meet quotas weighed heavily on my mind. Yet, despite these uncertainties, there was an inexplicable allure to the challenge—a sense that if I could master this skill, it would open doors I hadn't even imagined.

I delved into every training program New York Life offered and sought guidance from successful mentors. Despite my best efforts, selling remained relentlessly tough. My self-talk didn't help either.

You're too young and have no experience, David. You haven't had any success. How do I even start?

These thoughts gnawed at my confidence, making each day feel like an uphill battle.

Fast forward 36 years to age 60. While I've honed my skills and become adept at sales, the challenge hasn't diminished. Even now, I think: *Am I still relevant in this rapidly changing market? Can I keep up with the younger, tech-savvy competitors? What if my tried-and-true methods become obsolete?* These thoughts, though different from my younger days, still push me to evolve and adapt.

Starting Trent Capital Management at age 33 was another uphill battle. Just when I thought I had figured it all out, strategies that once worked suddenly stopped yielding results. I vividly remember a pivotal moment in 2022 when I suggested our new access to alternative investments portfolios to a long-time client, the CEO of a mid-sized company.

"David," he said, leaning back in his chair, "I've always valued your advice, but I'm not sure this aligns with our current goals."

I felt a familiar knot in my stomach, reminiscent of my early days at New York Life. I spent weeks with my team tailoring this presentation, confident it would resonate. Yet here I was, watching my carefully crafted advice fall flat.

Later that evening, I couldn't shake off the feeling of disappointment.

Maybe I'm losing my touch. Or maybe the market has changed more than I realized.

But then, a spark of determination ignited within me.

No, this is just another challenge. I've faced setbacks before, and I'll overcome this one too.

It was a stark reminder that in sales, and especially in financial services, you can never rest on your laurels. The market, client needs, and strategies are in constant flux, demanding continuous learning and adaptation.

This cycle of discovery, setback, and reinvention has been a constant in my entrepreneurial journey. I've coined it as FSO—figuring stuff out. It's been a rollercoaster of frustrations, successes, and lessons learned. But through it all, I've discovered the immense joy and growth that comes from tackling things head-on.

Every setback I faced was followed by a relentless comeback fueled by tenacity and a refusal to accept defeat. The process of overcoming obstacles, innovating, and adapting shaped my professional success and molded me into a more resilient and confident individual.

The essence of doing hard things daily seeped into every aspect of my life. It's a constant reminder that growth and success are often born out of challenges. Even when faced with failures, the resilience gained from pushing through tough times has been my guiding light.

I realize the journey of entrepreneurship and sales isn't just about achieving success but also about embracing the process, learning from failures, and continually evolving. It's about embracing the discomfort of uncertainty and using it as a catalyst for growth and innovation.

As I reflect on my 36-year journey, I can't help but smile. *Who would have thought that a scared 24-year-old would still be here, still learning, still growing? But here I am, ready for whatever challenge comes next.*

FAMILY VALUES
A Sack of Potatoes: The Unforgettable Sales Pitch

Imagine my good friend and business-savvy nephew, Marlon Haynes, and Ryan Woolard. The tale begins in nephew Ryan's high school days when he sought to make some extra money. That's when I connected him with Marlon, whose offices overlooked a busy basketball gym and workout center.

Marlon excelled in two areas: sports training and commercial janitorial services. Ryan, on the other hand, became a jack-of-all-trades in Marlon's world handling maintenance, deliveries, and even assisting with basketball training while keeping the offices tidy. The variety of tasks kept Ryan on his toes.

As Ryan learned the ins and outs of Marlon's business, a new opportunity arose—delving into sales for Marlon's janitorial company, 21st Century Janitorial. Marlon, being wise, provided Ryan with a list of contacts to reach out to. Here's where the fun begins. Marlon, with his quirky charm, scripted Ryan's cold calls with a memorable introduction: "Hi, I'm Ryan Woolard. You don't know me from a sack of potatoes."

I remember the first time Ryan told me about this script. We sat in my living room, and I watched him fidget.

"Uncle David," he said, looking up at me with wide eyes, "Marlon wants me to start my calls with 'You don't know me from a sack of potatoes.' What does that even mean?"

I chuckled, trying to reassure him. "It's just Marlon's way of breaking the ice, Ryan. It's quirky, but it might just work. People remember things that make them laugh."

Ryan sighed, still unsure. "I don't know, it feels so weird. What if they just hang up on me?"

As he voiced his concerns, I saw the anxiety in his eyes. I thought back to my own early days in sales, feeling that same knot in my stomach before every call. "Ryan," I said, placing a hand on his shoulder, "the worst they can do is say no. And if they do, you move on to the next call. But if you make them laugh, you've already won half the battle."

Intrigued by this amusing phrase, I decided to explore its origins. It turns out, "you don't know me from a sack of potatoes" is a whimsical idiom, poking fun at someone's lack of familiarity. Rooted in colloquial expressions, it evolved over time to add humor to everyday conversations.

While the phrase didn't exactly skyrocket Ryan's sales efforts (no surprises there), it did give us a funny story and a gentle reminder that a touch of humor can make business, and life in general, more enjoyable and memorable.

One evening, after a particularly tough day of calls, Ryan called me. "Uncle David," he said, his voice tinged with frustration, "I think I've been hung up on more times today than I can count. Maybe this whole 'sack of potatoes' thing isn't working."

I could hear the defeat in his voice. "Ryan, sales is tough, and rejection is part of the game. But remember, every 'no' brings you closer to a 'yes.' And sometimes, it's not about the script but how you connect with people. Keep your head up and keep trying. You'll find your rhythm."

As I hung up the phone, I couldn't help but feel a mix of pride and empathy. Ryan was learning the hard lessons of sales, just as I had. But he also discovered the importance of resilience and the value of a good sense of humor.

I realize moments like these, filled with quirky scripts and heartfelt conversations, truly shape our journey. They remind us that while success is important, it's the relationships we build and the laughter we share that make the journey worthwhile.

MASTER TEACHINGS
The Transformative Power of Enthusiasm
and Resilience in Sales

During the early stages of my career in sales and business development, I stumbled upon a life-changing read: Frank Bettger's *How I Raised Myself from Failure to Success in Selling*, published in 1947. I remember the day I first picked up the book, feeling lost and discouraged after another failed sales pitch.

What am I doing wrong? There has to be a secret to this, something I'm missing.

Bettger's story is captivating—starting as a failed insurance salesman at 29 but transforming into a successful estate owner ready for retirement by the age of 40. As I read his words, I felt a glimmer of hope. *If he could do it, maybe I can too.*

This book quickly became my trusted companion, a well-worn guide I frequently revisited to refine my skills and master the fundamentals of sales. I reached for it after a tough day, seeking wisdom and encouragement.

Bettger's teachings serve as a roadmap to achieving sales success. One crucial lesson that deeply resonated with me is the power of enthusiasm. He emphasizes the importance of genuinely being passionate about one's product or service, highlighting how this enthusiasm is infectious and can sway hesitant prospects into becoming eager customers.

I can still hear Bettger's words echoing in my mind: "Enthusiasm is by far the highest paid quality on Earth, probably because it is one of the rarest; yet it is one of the most contagious."

This concept hit me like a lightning bolt. *It's not just about knowing the product,* I realized. *It's about believing in it, living it, breathing it.* I made it a central principle in my approach, infusing every pitch with genuine excitement.

Another vital concept from Bettger is the art of building relationships. He emphasizes the significance of trust and rapport in sales, affirming that people are more likely to buy from those they know, like, and trust.

"The best way to sell yourself to others is first to sell the others to yourself," Bettger writes. This philosophy resonated deeply, and changed how I viewed my interactions with clients.

I integrated this philosophy, and prioritized active listening, empathy, and understanding. I remember one particular client meeting where I consciously focused on building rapport rather than pushing for a sale.

To my surprise, the client opened up about his business, and we ended up having a meaningful conversation that led to a long-term partnership.

Bettger also emphasizes the importance of persistence and resilience in sales. His personal journey of bouncing back from failures reminds me to persevere and learn from setbacks.

"Every failure brings with it the seed of an equivalent success," Bettger asserts. This mindset of resilience was pivotal and pushed me to keep going even during challenging times.

I recall a particularly tough period when I faced rejection after rejection. Feeling defeated, I turned to Bettger's book once again. His words gave me strength: "How you think when you lose determines how long it will be until you win."

Okay, David, these rejections are just steps in the process. Learn from them, adjust, and keep moving forward.

Furthermore, Bettger's book delves into effective communication and persuasion techniques. His insights on delivering compelling presentations enhanced my ability to influence and persuade. I started structuring my pitches differently, focusing on the client's needs rather than just listing product features.

In essence, *How I Raised Myself from Failure to Success in Selling* is not just a book; it's a timeless blueprint for achieving sales triumph. Its wisdom on enthusiasm, relationship-building, resilience, and communication continues to shape my sales strategy and overall business approach.

Even now, decades into my career, I find myself returning to Bettger's teachings. Each time I open the book, I'm reminded of that young, uncertain salesman I once was, and I'm grateful for the guidance that helped shape me into the professional I am today.

Thank you, Frank, your lessons have been invaluable, and they continue to inspire and guide me every day.

TRENT TAKEAWAYS

- Make your future bigger than your past.

- Figure out a way.

- Step out of your comfort zone and tackle hard things.

"Never underestimate the power of an encouraging word."

~John Maxwell

CHAPTER 3

ENCOURAGE

ENTREPRENEURIAL INSPIRATION

The Ripple Effect of Mentorship: How Timely Words and Unwavering Support Can Transform Careers and Lives

The power of encouragement has been a driving force throughout my life and career journey. From overcoming self-doubt to achieving milestones I once thought impossible, encouragement has been the catalyst for my growth and success.

I mentioned in Chapter 1 crossing paths with Bob Hamilton, a seasoned mentor whose guidance shaped my early professional years. Bob, having carved his own path in the insurance and benefits realm after a successful stint at New York Life, graciously took me under his wing.

During my time with Bob, I had the honor of meeting Dick Cobb, a pivotal figure whose influence resonates profoundly with me to this day. Not only did Dick offer me a position at New York Life, but he also assumed the role of my sales manager and a beacon of inspiration. His knack for motivation and mentorship was unparalleled, earning him a well-deserved spot in the Hall of Fame for encouragement.

Our weekly performance review and planning sessions, fondly referred to as PRP, were a testament to Dick's unique approach—a delicate balance of accountability and enduring support. One memorable session stands out.

"David," Dick began, looking me straight in the eye, "I know this week was tough, but remember, every setback is a setup for a comeback. Let's break down what happened and figure out how we can turn it around."

His words were a lifeline, pulling me out of the depths of self-doubt and reigniting my drive. I remember sitting there, feeling the weight of the week's failures pressing down on me.

Why can't I get this right?

Frustration bubbled up inside. But Dick's calm demeanor and unwavering belief in my potential made me pause and reconsider.

"Okay, let's do this," I replied, my voice tinged with a mix of determination and uncertainty. We spent the next hour dissecting each interaction, identifying what went wrong and brainstorming ways to improve. Dick's genuine belief in my ability to bounce back made a huge difference.

Navigating building a career at New York Life was no easy feat, yet Dick's influence proved invaluable. His guidance instilled in me the significance of cultivating daily and weekly habits, such as setting clear goals, maintaining a disciplined schedule, and consistently following up with clients. These habits had a profound impact on my personal and professional development.

I recall one particular conversation with Dick that left a lasting impression. "David," he said, "success isn't about grand gestures or overnight achievements. It's about the small, consistent actions you take every day. Keep your eye on the long-term goal but focus on winning each day."

This pivotal period marked a turning point. I shifted from merely surviving to thriving, understanding that success was a result of consistent effort and strategic planning. Bob and Dick created a ripple effect with their encouragement. It not only shaped my path but also inspired a culture of growth and achievement. Their legacy continues to guide me, reinforcing the belief that encouragement isn't just a gesture but a catalyst for transformative progress and fulfillment in both life and career.

Today, I strive to pay it forward. For instance, when a mentee recently struggled with a major client presentation, I sat down with him and said, "I believe in your potential. Let's work through this together and make it a success."

As we worked on his presentation, I saw the anxiety in his eyes. "What if I mess up?" he asked, his voice shaky.

"Remember, every great presenter started where you are now. It's not about being perfect; it's about being prepared and passionate. Let's focus on what you want to convey and how you can connect with your audience."

We spent hours refining his presentation, practicing his delivery, and building his confidence. The result was a successful presentation that boosted his confidence and performance.

Encouragement, I've learned, is about believing in others and helping them see their own potential. It's about being there in moments of doubt and providing the support and guidance needed to turn setbacks into comebacks. The ripple effect of mentorship is powerful, and I'm grateful for the lessons Bob and Dick imparted to me. Their influence continues to shape my approach to both business and life, reminding me that the true measure of success isn't just in personal achievements but in the impact we have on others.

FAMILY VALUES
Lessons in Resilience: How Pee-Wee Football and a Father's Encouragement Shaped My Journey Through Adversity

Growing up in Rose City, North Little Rock, Arkansas, my childhood was marked by a memorable journey into pee-wee football. The year was 1970, and at the tender age of seven, I was immersed in a world of full pads, bright yellow jerseys adorned with the name Superwood, and a drill that seems somewhat outrageous by today's standards.

Picture two lines of young players charging at each other with a fervor only kids on a football field can muster. Helmets on, the collision was real, leaving us with a mix of adrenaline and excitement after every clash. Those were the days when safety measures were different, and the thrill of the game was paramount.

I remember my first day on the field, feeling both excited and terrified.

What if I'm not good enough? I thought to myself, my heart racing as I put on my oversized helmet. *What if I get hurt?*

Amidst the excitement of the game, my father, Howard, stood out as a constant source of support and encouragement. Despite me being far and away the smallest kid on the team, his consistent presence at nearly every practice was a testament to his dedication as a parent and a coach. His belief in my abilities, even when I doubted myself, was resolute. He saw talent, speed, and passion where others might have seen limitations.

"David, you may be small, but you're quick as lightning!" he'd call out during practice. "Use that speed, son. You can outrun them all!"

His words echoed in my mind as I lined up for drills, giving me the courage to face opponents twice my size. *I'm small, but I'm fast*, I'd repeat to myself, like a mantra. *I can do this.*

As I lined up for another drill, feeling small and out of place, I noticed a new teammate joining our group. He was everything I wasn't—big, strong, and tan, with piercing blue eyes that seemed to radiate confidence. I later learned his name was Greg McKenzie.

"Hey there, Tiger!" Greg called out, flashing a friendly smile. "Ready to show these guys what you've got?"

I was taken aback by his enthusiasm and kindness. "I. . . I'm not sure I belong here," I stammered.

Greg's blue eyes sparkled with determination. "Are you kidding? You're quicker than all of us put together! Come on, I'll race you to the end zone!"

As we sprinted across the field, I felt a surge of energy I hadn't experienced before. Greg's infectious personality and encouragement made me feel like I belonged, despite our physical differences.

After practice, as we gathered our gear, Greg approached me again. "You know, Tiger," he said, his voice filled with sincerity, "you've got something special. Don't let anyone tell you otherwise."

I looked up at him, feeling a mix of gratitude and admiration. "Thanks, Greg. You're a fantastic football player. I really look up to you."

He laughed, patting me on the back. "We're teammates now, buddy. We'll push each other to be better."

As I walked home that day, I couldn't stop smiling. *Maybe I do belong here after all. If someone like Greg believes in me, maybe I should believe in myself too.*

Throughout our childhood, Greg and I became great friends. His kindness and encouragement were constant reminders that strength comes in many forms. Even years later, I can still hear his enthusiastic voice cheering me on, "Let's go, Tiger Trent! You got this!"

Greg's friendship taught me the power of lifting others up, a lesson that shaped not only my approach to sports but also my future in business and mentoring. His infectious enthusiasm and support were living examples of how positivity can transform someone's experience and self-perception.

"Let's go Tiger Trent! You got this!" My father gave birth to the nickname, a moniker that embodied the tenacity and fearlessness he saw in me. His words of encouragement weren't just words; they were a catalyst for self-belief and confidence.

Each night after practice, my father told me, "David, you're capturing everyone's attention! You're fearless and tenacious, even though you're the smallest kid on the field. They're calling you Tiger Trent, and all of Rose City is talking about you!"

Those words ignited a fire within me. I laid in bed, and repeated to myself: *David, this is amazing! Everyone is raving about me, and I can't wait to get back to practice and continue to work on my craft.* This experience planted the seeds of self-belief and determination that shaped my future.

The impact of encouragement, especially when it comes from a loved one like a parent, cannot be overstated. It's a reminder that words have power, and belief in oneself can move mountains. The lessons learned in those early football days have become a blueprint for resilience, determination, and the importance of nurturing the potential in others.

Today, when I mentor one of my clients and I'm able to see what they can't see about themselves, I realize how important it is to tell them—to not keep it in my head but be a mirror of their unique strengths and encourage them to see that in themselves. And every time I encourage one of my clients, I give that gift of a reminder back to myself.

I recently worked with a young entrepreneur who was doubting his business plan. I saw the same fear and self-doubt in his eyes that I once had as a small kid on that football field.

"Chris," I said, channeling my father's spirit, "you have a unique vision here. You're ready and you have a great game plan! You've got the skills; now let's put them into action."

Seeing his confidence grow reminded me of the power of those encouraging words from my childhood. As I watched Chris straighten his shoulders and a spark of determination light up his eyes, I thought: *This is what Dad did for me. This is how we change lives, one word of encouragement at a time.*

MASTER TEACHINGS
The Transformative Power of Encouragement: Building Connections Through Carnegie's Principles

Dale Carnegie's *How to Win Friends and Influence People* isn't just a book to me; it's been a life-changing guide I've cherished since my younger days and continue to draw inspiration from. Carnegie isn't just another author on my shelf; he's a beacon of wisdom and insight. I've studied, absorbed, and applied his insights in countless situations.

For instance, I recall a pivotal moment during a client meeting with Matthew, a small business owner who struggled to adapt during the pandemic. As I listened to him express his concerns about maintaining his client base, I realized this was a perfect opportunity to apply Carnegie's principles.

"David, I'm just not sure how to keep my customers engaged," Matthew said, his voice tinged with frustration. "Everything's changed, and I feel like I'm losing touch with them."

I saw the worry etched on his face, and I thought back to Carnegie's teachings. *This is it. This is where I can make a difference.*

"Matthew," I began, leaning in to show my genuine interest, "you've done an incredible job building your community during these tough times. You've built trust, and that is key to success."

His eyes widened, and a small smile crept onto his face. "You really think so?" he asked, a hint of hope in his voice.

"Absolutely. Your dedication to your customers is evident, and that's something not everyone can achieve. Let's build on that strength."

Think about a world where every conversation or interaction is a chance to uplift and empower others. That's the transformative magic of Carnegie's lessons on the profound impact of encouragement. In Carnegie's universe, encouragement isn't merely a nicety but a potent force that can transform lives. It's about understanding the human psyche, recognizing the potential in others, and igniting that spark of confidence and motivation.

One of Carnegie's key principles is the importance of giving sincere and specific praise. It's not just about saying, "Good job," but about highlighting the specific actions or qualities that deserve commendation.

With Matthew, it sounded like this: "Matthew, you did a great job building your client base during the pandemic. You built trust, and that is key to success." I could see his face light up as he absorbed the recognition, and I felt a sense of fulfillment knowing I acknowledged his hard work.

Furthermore, Carnegie emphasizes the power of listening and showing genuine interest in others. By actively listening to their concerns, goals, and aspirations, we demonstrate empathy and create a supportive environment where individuals feel valued and understood.

In active listening, you're in it to understand not just what the person says, but how they feel and what the passion is behind what they're saying. When you actively listen, you're present, aware, and not thinking about what you'll say next. Your sole goal is to listen.

During my conversation with Matthew, I made a conscious effort to maintain eye contact, nod in understanding, and ask follow-up questions that encouraged him to share more about his experiences.

"Tell me more about what your customers have been saying," I prompted, genuinely curious.

Matthew seemed to relax, his shoulders easing. "Well, many of them are worried about the future. They want to feel secure and valued."

"That makes sense," I nodded. "How have you been addressing those concerns?"

Another aspect of Carnegie's teachings is the art of constructive feedback. Instead of criticizing or pointing out flaws, he advocates for offering feedback in a constructive and encouraging manner. This involves focusing on solutions, highlighting areas of improvement, and providing actionable steps for growth.

For instance, during a team meeting, I noticed that my colleague Sarah was struggling with her presentation skills. Rather than simply pointing out her nervousness or lack of clarity, I approached her afterward and said, "Sarah, I really appreciated your insights during the meeting. You have a great understanding of the material. If you'd like, I can share some tips on structuring your presentations to make them even more impactful. Practicing a few key points could help you feel more confident and engage our clients better."

Sarah's eyes lit up with gratitude. "Thank you, David. I'd really appreciate that."

This approach not only addressed my observations but also encouraged her to develop her skills and build her confidence.

Moreover, Carnegie underscores the importance of maintaining a positive attitude and mindset. Encouragement flourishes in an environment of optimism and belief in possibilities. By cultivating a positive outlook and projecting confidence, we inspire others to see challenges as opportunities and setbacks as stepping stones to success.

In those moments with Matthew, I realized my words had the potential to shape his perspective and motivate him to take action. I thought about how often we underestimate the impact of our encouragement and how a few sincere words can foster resilience and determination in others.

It's amazing how just a little bit of encouragement can go a long way.

In essence, Dale Carnegie's teachings on the power of encouragement revolve around lifting others up, recognizing their potential, and creating a supportive atmosphere where growth and success thrive. It's about harnessing the transformative power of words and actions to inspire, motivate, and empower individuals to reach their fullest potential.

As I continue to apply these principles in my daily interactions, I'm reminded of the profound impact they've had on my journey. Encouragement is not just a tool; it's a way of life that fosters connection, growth, and success.

TRENT TAKEAWAYS

- Increasing contributions to others is essential for lifetime growth.

- MOFI—Make Others Feel Important.

- Encouragement empowers, uplifts, and transforms lives.

CHAPTER 4

DUTY

ENTREPRENEURIAL INSPIRATION

Embracing the DUTY: How the Mailing List Approach Transformed My Sales Strategy and Built Lasting Connections

As I embarked on my journey with New York Life, the pressure of the "eat what you kill" compensation model was significant. Every sale was not just a financial gain but a lifeline in this high-stakes environment. It was during this time that my mentor and sales manager, Dick Cobb, introduced me to a transformative strategy known as the "mailing list approach," a cornerstone of New York Life's prospecting methodology.

The mailing list approach wasn't just about cold calls; it was a strategic dance of communication and connection. Armed with a concise script, I reached out to friends, referrals, and even strangers, inviting them for a 20-minute meeting to add them to my mailing list.

"Hi, this is David Trent from New York Life. I hope you're doing well! I'm reaching out to share some valuable information that could benefit you and your family. I'd love to set up a quick 20-minute meeting to discuss how I can help. Would you be available this week?"

At first, I was skeptical. *Who would want to meet with me just to get on a mailing list?* But Dick's confidence in the method was unwavering.

"David," he said one afternoon, "this isn't just about making calls. It's about creating opportunities to connect. Trust the process."

It may have seemed unorthodox, but its effectiveness was nothing short of magical. After implementing this approach, I saw my appointment bookings double, leading to a significant increase in my sales numbers and a growing network of potential clients.

New York Life's training emphasized the "DUTY" of booking three appointments daily. This disciplined routine freed me from the anxiety of uncertain sales and redirected my focus to the proactive pursuit of appointments. *Duty* became more than a word; it was a guiding principle that reshaped my approach to work and life.

As I immersed myself in this method, I witnessed its ripple effects. Beyond boosting my sales numbers, it instilled a sense of purpose and structure in my daily activities. Each appointment wasn't just a potential sale but an opportunity to connect, understand needs, and provide value.

In one particular meeting I listened to a potential client share her financial worries. She was a single mother, anxious about securing her children's future.

"David, I just don't know how I'll manage if something happens to me," she confided, her voice trembling.

I leaned in, feeling the weight of her concerns. "I understand, and I'm here to help. Let's work through this together and find a solution that gives you peace of mind."

By the end of our conversation, I hadn't only addressed her concerns but also started a relationship based on trust and understanding. I left that meeting feeling a profound sense of fulfillment.

This is what it's all about, making a real difference in people's lives.

What struck me most was how this approach transcended the professional realm. It taught me the power of consistency, persistence, and the art of building relationships. It wasn't just about closing deals; it was about nurturing connections and earning trust. I began to see every interaction as a chance to uplift others, reflecting Dale Carnegie's teachings.

As I navigated through this transformative experience, I reflected on the deeper meaning of my work.

Am I merely chasing numbers, or am I genuinely making a difference in people's lives?

Each successful appointment brought a sense of accomplishment, but I realized the true fulfillment came from the connections I built.

I thought about how I could further enhance my approach, ensuring that every interaction was meaningful and impactful. *How can I be more than just a salesperson? How can I become a trusted advisor, someone who truly cares about the financial well-being of my clients?*

Over time, the mailing list approach became second nature, a rhythm of outreach and engagement that fueled my growth and success. It taught me that taking proactive action, even in the face of uncertainty, is the key to progress. I'm grateful for the lessons learned and the foundation laid for a thriving career and a fulfilling life during those early days.

Reflecting on those moments, I realize that the "DUTY" of booking appointments was more than a task; it was a commitment to building lasting connections and making a positive impact. It was about embracing the responsibility to serve and support others, a principle that continues to guide me in all my endeavors.

FAMILY VALUES
Guided by Wisdom: How Simple Lessons Shape Our Journey Toward Purpose

During the years from two to five, my son Carter attended daycare at the Chenal Valley Church. It was an incredible place with exceptional teachers and caregivers.

I used to drop Carter off at Chenal Valley Church every morning. As we walked through the doors, I felt a mix of emotions—pride in my growing boy and a tinge of guilt for leaving him. *Will he be okay without me?*

The pastor's office was situated just about 20 feet to the left, and the pastor's name was Mr. Danny. He was a tall, super friendly, and boisterous man.

Whenever Carter walked in, Mr. Danny enthusiastically called out, "Carter, come here man!"

Carter's face instantly lit up, and he rushed over to Mr. Danny, jumping into his lap. I watched, amazed at how quickly my shy boy transformed in Mr. Danny's presence. *How does he do that?* I marveled silently.

Mr. Danny exchanged a few words with Carter before gently setting him down. "How's my favorite little man today?" he'd ask, and Carter would giggle in response.

As Carter walked away, he always said something that has stayed with me all these years: "Carter, (then pause as Carter looked back) do your duty."

The first time I heard it, I was taken aback. *Do your duty? What an odd thing to say to a child,* I thought. But as I pondered it on my drive to work, the depth of those simple words began to sink in.

This simple yet profound message resonated deeply with me. It encapsulated the essence of responsibility, commitment, and purpose. "Do your duty" wasn't just about fulfilling obligations; it was about embracing life with intentionality and dedication.

As I navigated my entrepreneurial journey I remembered those words. They became a mantra, guiding my actions and decisions. Whether it was booking three appointments daily or nurturing client relationships, I approached each task with a sense of duty and purpose.

One particularly tough day, when I was tempted to cut corners, I heard Mr. Danny's voice in my head: *David, do your duty.* It was the push I needed to stay the course.

The lessons I learned from Mr. Danny's words extended beyond the professional realm. They influenced how I parented, approached relationships, and lived my life. "Do your duty" became a philosophy—a reminder to act with integrity, kindness, and diligence in all aspects of life.

I remember one evening, exhausted after a long day, when Carter asked me to read him a bedtime story. My first instinct was to make an excuse, but then I thought, *this is my duty as a father.* So, I sat down, pulled him close, and began to read.

I'm grateful for Mr. Danny's wisdom and the transformative impact those three words had. They serve as a constant reminder that embracing our responsibilities and commitments with dedication and sincerity is the key to living a fulfilling and purpose-driven life.

Years later, I ran into Mr. Danny at a community event. "You probably don't remember," I said, "but your words to Carter every morning, 'do your duty,' they changed my life."

Mr. Danny smiled warmly. "I'm glad," he said. "That's my duty—to plant seeds that grow long after they leave our care."

As I walked away, I thought: *And now it's my duty to pass on this wisdom to others. The cycle of duty never really ends. It just grows and touches more lives along the way.*

MASTER TEACHINGS
From Doubt to Determination:
The Power of Duty in Achieving Success

Earl Nightingale's profound words from his book *Lead the Field* stuck in my mind as I navigated through life's ups and downs. His wisdom resonated deeply, reminding me of the importance of embracing duty as a source of joy and fulfillment.

I vividly remember a pivotal moment in my career when I decided to expand my wealth management team at Trent Capital Management. The firm had been growing steadily, but I realized that to truly elevate our services and reach more clients, I needed to bring in talented individuals who shared our vision.

As I sat in my office, contemplating the hiring process, doubts began to creep in.

What if I choose the wrong candidates?

My stomach churned.

What if they don't fit our culture? Can I really lead a larger team effectively?

I leaned back in my chair, closing my eyes and taking a deep breath. *Come on, David. You've faced challenges before. Why is this one so daunting?*

However, Nightingale's teachings urged me to approach the situation with a sense of duty and purpose. I recalled his assertion that "success is the progressive realization of a worthy ideal." This perspective shifted my focus from my fears to the opportunity at hand.

I could almost hear Nightingale's voice: "David, remember, duty isn't a burden. It's an opportunity to grow, to prove yourself, to make a difference."

Drawing inspiration from Nightingale's favorite poem by Robert Degaure, I realized life wasn't just about seeking joy and happiness; it was about embracing duty wholeheartedly. I shifted my perspective, seeing duty not as a burden but as an opportunity for growth and fulfillment.

This is my chance to prove myself, straightening up in my chair. *To rise to the occasion and show what I can do.*

With renewed determination, I delved into the project, fully engaging myself in the work at hand. I organized meetings with the teams, clarified expectations, and fostered open communication. Instead of viewing it as a chore, I saw it as a steppingstone toward my goals, a journey that led me to greater achievements and personal satisfaction.

During one of these meetings, a team member asked, "David, how do you stay so motivated through this process?"

I smiled, thinking of Nightingale's words. "I've learned to see duty as a source of joy," I replied. "Each challenge is an opportunity to grow and excel."

Then, something remarkable happened. The more I dedicated myself to my duty, the more joy and fulfillment I felt. It wasn't just about reaching the end goal; it was about relishing every step of the journey and learning along the way. Each small victory, each resolved conflict, became a source of motivation.

I never thought I'd feel this energized by such a demanding process, I mused one evening, reflecting on the day's progress.

Nightingale's teachings had a profound impact on my mindset. I began to see duty as a source of joy, a pathway to personal growth, and a reflection of my commitment to excellence. It transformed how I approached tasks, relationships, and life in general. I realized that by embracing my responsibilities, I was not only growing professionally but also finding deeper satisfaction in my work.

In the end, I realized true happiness and fulfillment come from doing our duty wholeheartedly, finding joy in the process, and making each moment count. Earl Nightingale's timeless wisdom continues to guide me, reminding me that duty, when embraced with passion and purpose, can indeed lead to joy and fulfillment in life.

As I successfully completed the expansion of our team, I sat back in my office, a sense of accomplishment washing over me. *Thank you, Earl,* quietly looking at his book on my shelf. *Your wisdom turned my doubt into determination, and my duty into joy.*

TRENT TAKEAWAYS

- The seed of money is service.

- ACT – Assume Challenges Today.

- How do I view duty—as a burden or as an opportunity for growth?

CHAPTER 5

PATH

ENTREPRENEURIAL INSPIRATION

From Commission to Confidence: Navigating the 'Eat What You Kill' Philosophy on My Path to Success

My time at New York Life spanned seven years, from 24 until I turned 31. The philosophy of "eat what you kill" was the norm, meaning I was 100% commission based. My income was a direct reflection of my hard work; for instance, in my first year, I earned around $30,000, but as I honed my skills and built my client base, that number grew to over $100,000 by my final year.

I remember my first day at New York Life, sitting at my desk, staring at the phone. *This is it.*

My heart raced.

My future depends on these calls.

I picked up the receiver, my hand trembling slightly.

Come on, David. You can do this. One call at a time.

This model instilled a true entrepreneurial spirit in me, as my financial success depended solely on my efforts and perseverance.

Over the past thirty-six years, from daunting events in my early days to the exhilarating triumphs that followed, I'm reminded of the important concept of being on a PATH. This idea wasn't just a metaphorical journey but a guiding principle deeply rooted in my experiences and the teachings of Earl Nightingale, particularly from his work *Lead the Field*.

Nightingale's definition of success as "the progressive realization of a worthy goal" resonated profoundly. It became my mantra, shaping my mindset to always perceive obstacles as steppingstones on my path to success.

Success is the progressive realization of a worthy goal, I'd repeat to myself during tough times. *I'm on the path, even if I can't see the destination yet.*

My goals during this time included building a robust client portfolio, mastering the intricacies of the investment world, and ultimately transitioning into a leadership role.

The early years were marked by relentless execution and a thirst for learning, leveraging the tools and knowledge provided by New York Life. Some strategies yielded immediate success, while others were valuable lessons in resilience and adaptability.

I remember a particularly tough month when I struggled to meet my appointment goals. Sitting at my desk, surrounded by rejection, I felt defeated.

What am I doing wrong?

I took a deep breath.

This is just a hurdle, and every setback is a setup for a comeback.

I embraced the uncertainties, always trusting in the concept of the PATH. No matter the hurdles, I found solace in knowing I was continually progressing toward my worthy goals.

One pivotal moment came at the age of thirty-one in 1994 when I transitioned from New York Life to Morgan Keegan, fully immersing myself in the investments arena. It was a leap of faith into the unknown; I had little experience in investments, and the thought of starting anew was daunting.

What if I fail? I wondered, standing in front of Morgan Keegan's intimidating building on my first day. But then I reminded myself: *Every experience and challenge are a part of my journey.* I knew each propelled me forward on my PATH.

I often shared this sentiment with colleagues, saying, "Embracing the unknown is where growth happens." I remember one particular conversation with a nervous new hire. "Listen," I told him, "I was in your shoes not too long ago. Trust the process, embrace the challenges. That's where the real learning happens."

The teachings of Earl Nightingale continued to resonate as I faced obstacles and celebrated victories. The concept of success being a progressive realization fueled my determination and perseverance.

I vividly recall a conversation with a mentor during a challenging project. As we pored over complex financial models late into the night, I felt overwhelmed. Sensing my frustration, he looked at me and said, "Remember, David, success isn't just about the end result; it's about the journey and what you learn along the way."

Those words stuck with me. With each setback, I grew stronger and more resilient, always embracing the fact that I was on a PATH leading to greater accomplishments and personal growth.

Now, as I reflect on the founding of Trent Capital Management and the years that followed, I'm grateful for the challenges, uncertainties, and victories that shaped my entrepreneurial journey.

Sitting in my office at Trent Capital, looking out the window, I often think back to that young man making his first cold calls at New York Life.

You did it, David: one step at a time, one challenge at a time, you built this.

The PATH reminds me: Success isn't just a destination but a continuous journey of progress and fulfillment. Each step, each decision, contributes to growth, reinforcing the idea that the journey itself is as valuable as the destination.

FAMILY VALUES

Lessons in Resilience: How My Father's Humble Beginnings Shaped His Perspective on Life and Work

Growing up, my dad, Howard Trent, experienced a unique childhood that shaped his perspective on life. He often reminisces about the house he grew up in, one of those quintessential "shotgun houses" on Baker Row.

"We had one of those simple houses where everything was close together," he would say, his eyes distant with memory. "Most people grew up with two bedrooms and a bath; we grew up with two rooms and a path."

I remember the first time he told me this, sitting on our porch one summer evening. I was complaining about sharing a room with my brother, and Dad's words stopped me in my tracks. "Two rooms and a path?" I thought, trying to imagine what that must have been like.

This encapsulated the simplicity and resourcefulness of their home. Their house consisted of one bedroom and a multipurpose room, lacking modern amenities like running water. Instead, they relied on an outhouse for their bathroom needs and fetched water from a well.

I often thought about my dad's determination when he had to use the outhouse. *He had no choice but to succeed in that journey to relieve himself and stay on that 'PATH'.* It struck me then how this simple, daily task was a metaphor for life. I approached my own goals with the same mindset—keep pushing forward and find resources, through people and books, to make it happen.

What they faced in their living situation wasn't just physical but also symbolic of the progression of resilience and adaptability instilled in them. Dad vividly describes the process of digging a six-foot-deep hole for the outhouse.

"We created a worn-down path to it through the grass," he explained, his voice a mix of amusement and pride. "Sometimes it was freezing cold going out there at night. And we had to watch out for the wasps that were attracted to the waste."

I remember shuddering at the thought. "Dad," I once asked, "weren't you scared going out there in the dark?"

He chuckled. "Sure, I was. But when you gotta go, you gotta go. Fear doesn't change that."

His words stuck with me, a reminder that sometimes, we have to face our fears head-on, no matter how unpleasant the task.

Moreover, the struggle extended to their water source, an 80-foot-deep well they could barely afford to dig. "It was a total embarrassment digging that hole during the day and then trying to relocate it at night when the old hole was full," Dad told us, his voice tinged with a mix of humor and remembering discomfort.

I could almost picture my young father navigating in the dark, trying to find the right spot. "How did you manage?" I asked, fascinated and horrified at the same time.

"You just did. There wasn't any other choice," he replied.

This necessary but humbling task highlighted the grit and determination required to navigate their circumstances. I thought about this when faced with my own challenges. *If Dad could handle that, surely I can handle this*, became my internal pep talk.

Despite the struggles, Dad's upbringing instilled in him a strong work ethic, resourcefulness, and gratitude for the simple things in life. His childhood experiences taught him valuable lessons about perseverance, problem-solving, and making the most out of what you have.

I remember one tough day at work, feeling overwhelmed and ready to give up. I called Dad, seeking advice. "Son," he said, his voice warm and reassuring, "remember where we came from. If we could make do with two rooms and a path, you can figure this out. Just keep moving forward."

These early hardships laid the foundation for his resilience and determination to face life's obstacles head-on. And through his stories and example, they became part of my foundation too. Every time I face a challenge, I think of that worn path to the outhouse, a symbol of perseverance and the willingness to do what needs to be done, no matter how difficult.

MASTER TEACHINGS
The Journey of Success: Embracing Progress Toward Worthy Ideals

Success, as Earl Nightingale articulates in *Lead the Field*, is not merely the attainment of a goal but the continual progression toward a worthy ideal. This definition resonates deeply, especially when considering the concept of a path as Webster defines it—a direction or course one is moving in, one's PATH, if you will.

I remember the first time I read Nightingale's words: "Success is the progressive realization of a worthy ideal." It hit me like a thunderbolt. *Wait,* I thought, *success isn't just about reaching the finish line? It's about the journey itself?* This revelation changed everything for me.

Growing up, I witnessed my father's steady commitment to his goals, whether he provided for our family or pursued his passions. His example taught me the importance of taking action and making consistent progress toward my own worthy ideals.

I recall a conversation with my father when I struggled with a challenging project at work. "Dad, I feel like I'm not getting anywhere. Like I'm failing."

He looked at me with understanding eyes and said, "It's not about the destination, it's about the journey. Are you moving forward, even a little bit each day?"

"Yeah, I guess I am," I replied, reflecting on the small progress I made.

"Then you're succeeding, son. Keep going."

It's not enough to dream or wish for success; one must actively work toward it with determination and discipline.

Nightingale's teachings emphasize that success is a journey, not a destination. This idea became ingrained in my mindset and shaped how I approach challenges and opportunities. Each step along the PATH is a chance to grow, learn, and move closer to realizing my aspirations.

I often find myself repeating Nightingale's words in my head: *Success is the progressive realization of a worthy ideal.*

What's fascinating about this concept is how it transforms one's perspective. As I've progressed on my own PATH, I've experienced firsthand the power of dedication and perseverance. Goals that once seemed distant or unattainable move within reach with consistent effort and a clear vision of what I want to achieve.

In 1999, I was overwhelmed by the ambitious goals I set for myself. I desperately wanted to grow my Trent Capital Management practice to the point where I was managing $25 million of clients' investments.

How will I ever get there?

Then I recalled Nightingale's teachings and shifted my focus.

It's not about getting there all at once. It's about making progress every day.

Moreover, Nightingale's definition of success encourages a broader understanding of what it means to lead a fulfilling life. It's not just about material accomplishments but also about personal growth, impact on others, and living in alignment with one's values and passions.

Applying these teachings, I've learned to set worthy ideals that go beyond mere financial success. Building meaningful relationships, making a positive impact on my community, and continuously improving myself are integral parts of my definition of success.

I shared this perspective with my colleagues during a meeting. "Success isn't just about our bottom line," I said. "It's about the value we create, the lives we touch, and how we grow as individuals and as a team."

Every morning, as I start my day, I ask myself: *What progress can I make today towards my worthy ideals?*

This simple question, inspired by Nightingale's teachings, keeps me focused and motivated, reminding me that success is not a distant goal, but something I can work toward every single day.

TRENT TAKEAWAYS

- Success is moving towards your goals. It's that simple.

- PUSH–Persist Until Something Happens.

- Do you look at obstacles as opportunities to test yourself?

"Curiosity about life in all of its aspects, I think,
is still the secret of great creative people."

~Leo Burnett

CHAPTER 6

CURIOUS

ENTREPRENEURIAL INSPIRATION

Embracing Curiosity: How a Passion for Learning Transformed My Journey in Investments and Shaped My Career

In 1991, my fourth year at New York Life, I was 28 when I unexpectedly discovered a passion that completely transformed my professional journey: the captivating realm of investments. It was a thrilling yet daunting period for me as I delved into the intricacies of this new venture, navigating through its complexities with determination and curiosity.

As I sat at my desk, poring over financial reports and market analyses, I felt excitement and trepidation.

What if I can't keep up? What if I make mistakes that cost my clients?

These inner doubts fueled my desire to learn and grow in this unfamiliar territory.

One pivotal moment was when I obtained my securities exam qualification, opening doors to selling mutual funds. As I held the certificate in my hands, a surge of pride and possibility washed over me.

"This is it," I whispered to myself. "This is my chance to make a real difference."

Inspired by the multifaceted services offered by New York Life agents, I saw an opportunity to not just sell investments but to truly assist clients in navigating the intricacies of finances and portfolio management.

However, I faced a common challenge: the daunting gap in experience and knowledge. Rather than succumbing to insecurity, I channeled my energy into curiosity and a thirst for learning. I vividly remember sitting down with my mentor, Dick Cobb, during one of our weekly meetings.

"Dick," I asked, leaning forward, "what resources do you recommend for someone just starting in investments?"

He smiled and pointed me toward some foundational texts and research services. "Start with the basics and build from there. Don't hesitate to ask questions—every expert was once a beginner."

His encouragement and guidance helped me understand that asking questions was a vital part of my growth. "It's okay not to know everything," I reminded myself. "The important thing is to keep learning."

Two key elements played a crucial role in helping me gain valuable experience in investing. The first was Morningstar, a premier research service providing comprehensive insights into mutual funds. The subscription fee was beyond my reach at the time, but I found an abundance of information at the public library.

I can still remember the excitement I felt as I walked into the library, heading straight for the finance section to pull out the hefty Morningstar binders. *This is where it all begins!*

Immersing myself, I spent countless hours absorbing details about various mutual funds. This deep dive not only enhanced my understanding of investments but also broadened my perspective on global economies and financial markets.

I also discovered *Mutual Funds for Dummies*. Despite its light-hearted title, the information was priceless in simplifying intricate investment ideas and tactics. As I flipped through the pages, I chuckled at some of the straightforward explanations. *If only I had found this sooner.*

The easy-to-understand language and useful tips laid a strong groundwork for my continuous learning in mutual funds and investment management. Thanks to this book, I stumbled upon many other fantastic reads that expanded my investments knowledge.

Armed with newfound knowledge and a growing passion for the investment world, I realized this journey is one of lifelong learning, and I kept that beginner's mindset throughout my career. Each discovery, whether through books, research services, or hands-on experience, contributed to my evolution as an investment advisor dedicated to serving clients with integrity and expertise.

One day, as I was explaining a complex investment strategy to a client, I caught myself using terms and concepts that would've baffled me just a few months earlier.

Look how far you've come! And there's still so much more to learn.

Those early days of curiosity and determination set the stage for a fulfilling and impactful career in the financial industry, driven by a relentless pursuit of knowledge and a commitment to helping clients achieve their financial goals.

As author Brian Herbert states, "The capacity to learn is a gift; the ability to learn is a skill; the willingness to learn is a choice."

I made that choice every day, and it has made all the difference.

FAMILY VALUES

Curiosity and Resilience: How My Dad's Journey in Truck Insurance Built a Lasting Family Legacy

The power of curiosity prevails in this tale of my dad's entry into the truck insurance world.

Dad cherishes the memory of selling his inaugural truck insurance policy in 1970. One day, Jim Smith, an employee at Dad's uncle's Mack Trucks dealership, approached him with a question: "What about insuring large trucks?"

I can imagine Dad's initial surprise, his mind racing with thoughts of uncertainty and excitement. *Truck insurance? I've never even considered that before*, he must've thought. But instead of backing away from the unknown, Dad's curiosity kicked in.

Although Dad had no prior experience, he boldly accepted the task. "Wow, I don't know, but it sounds like a great idea. Let's figure this out!" Dad replied, determined to learn everything he could.

I often wonder about that moment, picturing Dad's eyes lighting up with the thrill of a new challenge. *That's the spark that changed our family's trajectory.* I marveled at how one curious response could alter a life's path.

Dad's first client for truck insurance was Raymond Dowdy, but unfortunately, he made a mess of the policy, and Dowdy left after just six months. I can almost hear Dad's disappointment: *I really messed that one up. Maybe I'm not cut out for this.* But then, his resilience kicked in.

However, Dad didn't let that discourage him. Instead, he used it as a learning experience, reflecting on his mistakes and how he could improve. "Every setback is just a setup for a comeback," he often said. Slowly but surely, his truck insurance business began to thrive, and to this day, Dad and Jim Smith remain close friends.

Selling truck insurance turned out to be quite lucrative for Dad. He started earning larger commissions than ever before, and some of his best clients included JJ Reeves, Wayne Phillips, Thomas Surrett, the Vaughn Brothers, Jim Higgins, Toe Daniels, and Terry Mason.

During the summers, once my brother Keith turned 16, he accompanied Dad on calls to truckers. If Dad made a sale, he would turn to Keith with a grin and say, "Alright, let's light up some cigars to celebrate our victory!"

I can picture Keith's excitement, feeling grown-up and part of something important. They enjoyed the celebratory cigars on the way home, much to Mom's dismay. "You know your mother won't be happy about this," Dad chuckled. But he and Keith cherished those memories.

I remember feeling a mix of envy and admiration when Keith returned from these trips, smelling of cigars and success.

One day, I'll be part of this too.

Dad was still in the truck insurance business at 87, serving around 25 clients. It became a family legacy. His youngest son, Steve, built a highly successful truck insurance business in Texas, following in Dad's footsteps and further solidifying the family's presence in the industry.

From Steve: "Growing up, I watched Dad build his truck insurance business from the ground up, and it inspired me to do the same. His dedication and passion for helping clients taught me that success isn't just about making money; it's about building relationships and a legacy that lasts."

Hearing Steve talk about Dad's influence always fills me with pride and a sense of continuity.

This is what family legacy looks like.

Dad's success in this field allowed the family to move to a more upscale area called Overbrook in North Little Rock, leaving behind our old home in Rose City. In 1978, Mom and Dad settled into their new address at 6012 Elk River. Terry attended Arkansas State University, and Keith started his freshman year at Southern Methodist University.

I remember the day we moved, feeling a mix of excitement for our new home and nostalgia for the old one.

This is what progress looks like.

We watched our belongings being loaded into the moving truck.

Keith often teases Steve and me that we can't truly claim to be from Rose City anymore. "You fancy Overbrook boys," he'd joke. But underneath the teasing, there was always a sense of pride in how far our family had come.

Thanks to the truck insurance business, Mom and Dad could afford to send all four kids to college. They made sure each child received a great education, which started yet another legacy within the Trent family.

I'm struck by how one curious decision by Dad set off a chain reaction that shaped our entire family's future.

Curiosity and resilience. That's the Trent family recipe for success.

MASTER TEACHINGS
Harnessing Curiosity and Focus:
The Keys to Unlocking Your Potential

Carol Dweck's groundbreaking work in her book *Mindset: The New Psychology of Success* sheds light on the interplay between curiosity, focus, and achievement. She introduces the concept of the growth mindset, where individuals view challenges as opportunities to learn and grow. This mindset fosters a healthy balance between curiosity-driven exploration and focused effort.

I remember the first time I picked up Dweck's book. I felt stuck. I attained success, but wanted to get to the next level.

Maybe this will help.

It solidified some of my earlier learnings and transformed my approach to life.

In the context of curiosity and focus, Dweck's teachings highlight the importance of channeling curiosity into meaningful pursuits. She emphasizes the need to cultivate a growth-oriented mindset that embraces challenges and seeks new knowledge. When curiosity is directed toward specific tasks or goals, it becomes a powerful catalyst for innovation and progress.

Dweck's research suggests that individuals with a growth mindset are more likely to persevere through obstacles and maintain focus on their objectives. They view setbacks as learning experiences and remain curious about finding solutions and improving their skills. As Dweck states, "In the growth mindset, failure can be a painful experience. But it doesn't define you. It's a problem to be faced, dealt with, and learned from."

I remember trying to add new clients without much success. I felt the familiar pang of failure creeping in—that knot in my stomach.

Why is this happening to me?

But then I recalled Dweck's words.

Failure doesn't define you, I reminded myself. *It's a problem to be faced, dealt with, and learned from.*

On the other hand, a fixed mindset, characterized by a fear of failure and a desire for validation, can hinder curiosity and focus. Individuals with a fixed mindset may be hesitant to explore new ideas or take risks, leading to a lack of progress and achievement.

The key takeaway from Dweck's teachings is that a growth mindset enables individuals to harness their curiosity effectively. They approach tasks with a sense of curiosity and enthusiasm, eager to learn and adapt. By maintaining focus on their goals and continuously seeking knowledge, they're able to make meaningful progress and achieve success.

Adopting a growth mindset has been transformative. I learned to embrace challenges rather than shy away from them. When faced with obstacles, I remind myself of Dweck's assertion that "The view you adopt for yourself profoundly affects the way you lead your life." This perspective allows me to tackle difficulties with resilience and creativity.

When I encounter setbacks in my career, instead of feeling defeated, I begin to see them as opportunities for growth.

I started asking myself questions like:

What can I learn from this experience?

How can I adapt my approach moving forward?

This shift in thinking improved my problem-solving skills and also enhanced my ability to innovate in my business practices.

I recall a conversation with a team member during a challenging time. "David," she said, "how do you stay so positive when things go wrong?"

I smiled, thinking of Dweck's teachings. "I try to see setbacks as learning opportunities," I replied. "It's not about avoiding failure; it's about learning from it and coming back stronger."

Moreover, realizing my abilities aren't fixed encouraged me to pursue new skills and knowledge actively. I now approach learning with enthusiasm, understanding that effort and perseverance are key components of success. As Dweck emphasizes, "It's not always the people who start out the smartest who end up the smartest." This has inspired me to invest in my personal development continually.

One day, while struggling to master a new skill, I felt the frustration building. *Maybe I can't get to the next level.*

Then I remembered Dweck's words: "It's not always the people who start out the smartest who end up the smartest." With renewed determination, I pushed through, knowing that my efforts would pay off.

In summary, Carol Dweck's insights from *Mindset: The New Psychology of Success* underscore the importance of cultivating a growth mindset to balance curiosity and focus. When curiosity is guided by a growth-oriented mindset, it becomes a driving force for personal and professional development, leading to greater achievement and fulfillment. Embracing this mindset has empowered me to navigate life's obstacles with confidence and pursue my goals with renewed vigor.

Adopting a growth mindset transformed my career and enriched my life. Thank you, Carol. Your teachings unlocked a world of possibilities for me.

TRENT TAKEAWAYS

- Be curious about yourself.

- Replace judgment with curiosity.

- How is your curiosity being directed?

BUILDING FOUNDATIONS

MY 30s AND 40s AT
TRENT CAPITAL MANAGEMENT

"If I have seen further, it is by standing on the shoulders of giants."

~Isaac Newton

CHAPTER 7

CLUES

ENTREPRENEURIAL INSPIRATION
Embracing Mentorship and Learning:
How the 'Don't Reinvent the Wheel' Philosophy
Fueled My Journey in Building
Trent Capital Management

After stumbling upon the captivating realm of investments, I became enamored and soon consumed by it. It was clear transitioning from working with an insurance company to a conventional investment firm was necessary. At 31, I made a bold decision to embark on a new career path, taking a leap of faith in 1994 when I joined Morgan Keegan, a renowned regional firm, as an investment broker.

I sat at my new desk on my first day at Morgan Keegan and felt a mix of excitement and trepidation.

Am I really doing this? Can I really start over at 31?

But deep down, I knew this was where my passion lay.

This is where I learned not to reinvent the wheel, which allowed me to build on the successes of others rather than starting from scratch.

The concept of "don't reinvent the wheel" (DRW) has been a guiding principle in my entrepreneurial journey. I started during my early years at New York Life, where I dove headfirst into personal development materials while navigating a straight commission job at just 24.

However, the pivotal DRW moment crystallized when I crossed paths with Larry Waschka at 32, a fellow entrepreneur running his successful fee-only Registered Investment Advisor (RIA) firm, Waschka Capital Investments. Larry's story was a beacon of light in the business world. He transitioned from a successful stint at Merrill Lynch to creating his own thriving firm, all while garnering immense respect and admiration in our community.

Sitting across from Larry during our initial meetings, I absorbed every word of his success story. His journey mirrored the DRW philosophy perfectly—he didn't reinvent the wheel but instead learned from established models, adapted them, and forged his path to success.

As I listened, I thought, *If Larry can do this, so can I. I just need to apply what he's learned and make it my own.* My heart raced with excitement at the possibilities.

"Larry, how did you make the transition from Merrill Lynch to your own firm?" I asked.

He smiled, his eyes twinkling with the memory. "David, it wasn't easy, but I didn't try to reinvent everything. I took what worked at Merrill and studied other successful independent advisors' practices, improved upon them, and made them my own. That's the key."

His openness in sharing his recipe for success fueled my ambition, leading me to establish Trent Capital Management a year later.

Following Larry's blueprint, I meticulously built my practice, integrating his strategies while making tweaks to suit my style and vision. The early years were arduous, marked by many setbacks.

One significant challenge occurred when I lost a major client due to a miscommunication about their investment strategy. I was devastated and questioned my abilities.

Perhaps this isn't the right path for me.

My confidence was shaken. However, I took it as a learning opportunity. I reached out to the client, apologized, and asked for feedback on how I could improve. "I value your trust," I told them. "And I want to learn from this mistake."

This not only helped me regain their trust but also taught me the importance of clear communication and active listening. With each hurdle, I learned, refined, and grew, gradually steering Trent Capital Management toward stability and success.

What amazed me later was discovering that Larry himself drew largely from inspiration from Bob Markman, a renowned wealth manager in Minneapolis. This interconnected web of mentorship and knowledge exchange exemplifies the DRW ethos—standing on the shoulders of giants, leveraging proven strategies, and innovating within established frameworks.

This chain of mentorship was like a relay race with each person passing on their knowledge, and all of us moving forward together.

In hindsight, embracing DRW wasn't about copying or mimicking but about leveraging collective wisdom and experience to accelerate growth and navigate the complexities of entrepreneurship. I continue to carry this lesson, emphasizing the power of learning from others' successes and failures to chart a path toward lasting achievement and impact.

As I looked at Trent Capital Management, I was filled with gratitude for the mentors who shared their wisdom.

Thank you, Larry. Your willingness to share your journey shaped mine in ways I could've never imagined.

FAMILY VALUES

Steve Trent: Empowered by Family and Mentorship: How Resilience and Strategic Relationships Drive Entrepreneurial Success

Steve Trent's entrepreneurial path is a shining example of how family support and mentorship can shape a journey. With me as his older brother and a seasoned entrepreneur, Steve embarked on his business venture in

2002, motivated by the entrepreneurial drive that runs in our family. At the age of 31, he delved into the world of long-haul truck insurance, founding his very own company, Southern Transportation Insurance.

I remember the day Steve called me, his voice a mix of excitement and nervousness. "Davey, I'm thinking about starting my own truck insurance company," he said. "Do you think I can do it?"

"Absolutely, Steve," I replied without hesitation. "You've got the drive and the passion. Plus, you've got us to support you every step of the way."

Harnessing the power of networking and mentorship, I connected Steve with three industry experts: Steve Brockington, Terry Burnett, and Greg Hatcher. Drawing insights from their experiences and principles, Steve laid the foundation for Southern Transportation Insurance. Despite encountering the initial hurdles common to startups, such as securing funding and establishing a client base, Steve's determination and resilience shone through. He often faced rejection from potential clients, but each "no" only fueled his desire to improve and adapt his approach.

"David, I got turned down again today," Steve said, frustration evident in his voice. "What am I doing wrong?"

"Steve, every no is just a step closer to a yes," I reassured him. "Keep learning, keep adapting. Remember, resilience is key."

A turning point in Steve's journey came in 2006 when he sought counsel from another mentor, Paul Haley, after losing a significant account to a competitor who used Sentry Insurance. This setback was a wake-up call for Steve, prompting him to push the boundaries and seek endorsement and the ability to place clients with Sentry Insurance. Despite facing rejections and hurdles, his steadfast persistence and relentless pursuit paid off, ultimately earning him an appointment to sell through Sentry, a significant achievement given their exclusive nature with only a handful of agents as approved producers in Texas.

I remember Steve calling me after he finally secured the appointment. "David, I did it! Sentry approved me as an official producer," he exclaimed, his voice brimming with pride.

"That's fantastic, Steve!" I replied, feeling a surge of pride myself. "I knew you could do it. This is just the beginning."

Steve's dedication and exceptional performance didn't go unnoticed. His remarkable track record led to his induction into Sentry's prestigious HAUL of Fame and culminated in being named the top national producer for the company in 2021. This recognition underscored Steve's ability to turn challenges into opportunities and achieve remarkable success in a competitive industry.

In a strategic move in 2016, Steve sold Southern Transportation Insurance to Triumph Financial, a game-changing decision. Leveraging Triumph Insurance's extensive resources, Steve witnessed a tenfold increase in his practice, a testament to his strategic vision and business acumen.

"It's incredibly important to build meaningful relationships," says Steve. "The foundation of my success has always been the roadmap our dad laid down for us. His guidance and support, along with our family's faith in Christ, have been instrumental in my journey."

Hearing Steve talk about Dad's influence always fills me with pride and a sense of continuity.

This is what family legacy looks like.

Steve's story exemplifies the transformative power of perseverance, strategic decision-making, and a steadfast commitment to excellence. His journey is a testament to the impact of family values and mentorship in driving entrepreneurial success.

Steve's achievements make me think about the conversations we had and what he overcame.

If Steve can turn his setbacks into success, so can I. I remind myself of this during tough times. His journey is a constant source of inspiration, not just for me, but for everyone in our family.

MASTER TEACHINGS
Don't Reinvent the Wheel—Dr. Ivan Misner.

Dr. Ivan Misner's insights on "don't reinvent the wheel" resonate deeply in the world of business, where the allure of innovation often overshadows the value of tried-and-true methods.

I remember the first time I heard Dr. Misner speak at a business conference. His words hit me like a thunderbolt: "Success leaves clues. Why start from scratch when you can learn from those who've already succeeded?"

In the realm of entrepreneurship, there's a tendency to believe we must forge entirely new paths to achieve success. However, this mindset can lead to unnecessary obstacles and setbacks. Dr. Misner wisely points out that we can benefit greatly by leveraging the knowledge and experience of those who've already navigated similar journeys.

As I sat in the audience, I thought about all the times I stubbornly tried to figure things out on my own. *How much time and energy could I have saved if I had just asked for help?*

Reinventing the wheel, in essence, means starting from scratch when solutions already exist. It's akin to trying to build a new car without utilizing the years of research and development that have gone into existing models. This approach not only wastes time and resources but also increases the likelihood of making avoidable mistakes.

I thought about Dr. Misner's words: "Why spend years making mistakes that others have already made and learned from? Learn from their experiences, and you'll progress much faster."

The danger of reinventing the wheel lies in the missed opportunities to learn from history. Dr. Misner emphasizes the importance of humility and openness to learning from others. While education is valuable, real-world experience provides invaluable insights that textbooks cannot replicate.

I recall a conversation I had with a young entrepreneur after one of Dr. Misner's talks. "But don't we need to be innovative to stand out?" he asked.

"Innovation doesn't always mean starting from zero," I replied, channeling Dr. Misner's teachings. "Sometimes, it's about taking what works and making it better."

By embracing the wisdom of seasoned professionals and industry veterans, we gain access to a treasure trove of knowledge. Their successes and failures serve as invaluable lessons that guide us in making informed decisions and avoiding common pitfalls.

In practical terms, this means seeking mentorship, analyzing case studies, and networking with peers who have relevant experience. It's about recognizing that innovation doesn't always mean starting from scratch; sometimes, it involves refining and improving existing methods.

I remember implementing this approach in my own business. Instead of trying to create a completely new marketing strategy, I reached out to successful entrepreneurs in my field. "What has worked for you?" I asked. Their insights saved me months of trial and error.

Ultimately, Dr. Misner's teachings remind us that success in business isn't solely about groundbreaking ideas but also about smart execution and learning from the collective wisdom of those who've gone before us. It's about standing on the shoulders of giants rather than trying to reinvent the wheel from scratch.

As I left the conference that day, Dr. Misner's words stayed with me: "Remember, every successful person you admire once stood where you are now. They learned from others, and now it's your turn to do the same."

These words became a mantra for me, guiding my decisions and approach to business. Whenever I face a new obstacle, I remind myself: *Don't reinvent the wheel. Someone has likely faced this before. Seek their wisdom.*

Dr. Misner's teachings have not only saved me countless hours and resources but have also connected me with a network of mentors and peers who continue to inspire and guide me. It's a powerful reminder that in the world of business, we're not alone in our journey, and there's immense value in learning from those who've walked the path before us.

TRENT TAKEAWAYS

- Surround yourself with successful individuals and pay attention.

- Learn from others who have faced failure.

- OPE—Other People's Experiences.

"Commitment leads to action. Action brings your dream closer."

-Marcia Wieder

CHAPTER 8

COMMIT

ENTREPRENEURIAL INSPIRATION

Navigating Choices: The Power of Independence and
Friendship in Shaping an Entrepreneurial Journey

Back in the early months of 1996, just shy of hitting the two-year mark at Morgan Keegan, I stood at a pivotal moment in my career. Fueled by ambition and a desire to make a difference, I was at a crossroads. Larry Waschka kickstarted it all. An entrepreneurial force to be reckoned with, Larry was the mastermind behind Waschka Capital Investments. His success and innovative model caught my attention, and he graciously shared his recipe for success.

I remember sitting across from Larry, absorbing every word. "David," he said, his eyes twinkling with enthusiasm, "the key is to create value for your clients in a way that's uniquely yours." As I listened, I felt excited. *This could be my chance to make a real impact.*

Enter Hunter East, a close friend from college and an early client. Hunter, already flourishing in the family banking business, shared my fascination with Larry's model. We both saw the potential for a fruitful partnership and meticulously crafted a detailed business plan under the banner of TEAM: Trent East Asset Management.

During one of our brainstorming sessions, I turned to Hunter and said, "I think we could really make a mark in this industry." I was excited and nervous.

Hunter replied, his eyes lighting up, "Absolutely! With our combined networks and expertise, we can create something special."

Crafting the business plan with Hunter was an enjoyable experience, filled with creativity and thoughtful discussions that strengthened our friendship. We spent several weeks on it, and the prospect of embarking on this journey together seemed incredibly exciting.

However, despite our young ages, we both possessed a certain wisdom that led us to the conclusion that it would be best not to proceed together. One evening, as we were reviewing our plans, I voiced a concern that was nagging at me.

"What if we face challenges that strain our friendship?" I pondered aloud. I was worried.

Hunter nodded, understanding the potential risks. "We need to make sure our friendship comes first," he replied, disappointed and relieved.

Ultimately, we recognized that our individual visions might be better pursued independently. It was a bittersweet realization, but one that we both knew was right.

In the end, we made the decision not to embark on the journey as partners. Instead, I launched Trent Capital Management as the sole owner, remaining dedicated to my vision and choosing to pursue my entrepreneurial dreams solo.

Launching my firm in 1996 wasn't easy. The early years were marked by relentless pressure. I faced mounting expenses, struggled to attract clients, and often worried about cash flow.

During sleepless nights, I laid awake, my mind racing. *How will I make this work?* However, my persistent commitment and determination kept me going. I focused on attracting clients, managing expenses efficiently, and navigating the complexities of entrepreneurship.

There was an invaluable lesson learned from the almost-partnership with Hunter. While a partnership could've provided initial support, my journey as a sole owner allowed me to fully embody my vision and resilience. It taught me that commitment is the bedrock of success in entrepreneurship.

In the early days of Trent Capital Management (TCM), Hunter East was more than a friend; he was a big cheerleader. Those initial years were grueling. Having Hunter's support was quite meaningful, encouragement amidst some hard times.

During a particularly tough quarter when I struggled to secure clients, Hunter often checked in. I remember one call vividly. My voice was heavy with frustration as I shared my struggles.

Hunter's voice came through the phone, full of encouragement. "You've got this! Just keep pushing forward." His words were like a lifeline, pulling me out of my doubts.

His belief in me helped me stay focused and motivated. I often thought, *If Hunter believes in me this much, I owe it to both of us to keep going.*

Hunter's entrepreneurial journey took an incredible turn when he played a crucial role in leading his family to a life-altering exit from their banking business, ultimately selling it for a substantial eight-figure sum—a true testament to his vision and determination.

When I heard the news, I was incredibly proud of my friend.

Look at us now! I remembered our late-night planning sessions from years ago. *We both found our paths, just not the one we initially imagined.*

It's a delightful twist in the tale where our paths intersect not just in friendship but also in the shared experience of navigating the unpredictable yet rewarding landscape of entrepreneurship.

This journey is about the essence of commitment, unwavering focus, and determination in navigating the complexities of entrepreneurship. It's a testament to the power of determination and the drive to turn obstacles into pathways toward achieving one's dreams.

I'm grateful for the friendship that has endured and the lessons learned along the way. Thank you, Hunter, your support and our shared experiences have shaped me more than you know.

FAMILY VALUES

From Struggle to Success: The Importance of Support and Self-Determination in Education

Growing up in a family that prioritized education and commitment, I learned invaluable lessons about perseverance and the power of dedication. My parents, despite their own limited educational backgrounds, were committed to providing us with opportunities for higher education.

My older sister, Terry, set a high bar by excelling academically and earning her mathematics degree from Arkansas State University. I remember feeling a mix of pride and pressure when she graduated. *Can I live up to that standard?*

Inspired by her success, my brother pursued electrical engineering at Southern Methodist University (SMU) with a generous financial aid package. Encouraged by his achievements, I also enrolled at SMU, initially following his footsteps in electrical engineering.

However, despite being a top student in high school, I struggled academically in college, facing the harsh reality of a 1.9 GPA (after two years) and academic probation. The financial burden on my parents, who committed to supporting my education, weighed heavily on me.

I can still recall the moment I received my grades. My heart sank as I stared at the numbers on the paper. *How did this happen?* A wave of shame and disappointment washed over me. *I'm letting everyone down.*

Rather than giving up or retreating to a local college, I committed to turning my academic path around. I spent nights agonizing over how to approach my parents. *They've sacrificed so much for me. I can't let them down.*

Finally, I gathered my courage and presented a comprehensive plan to my parents, outlining my intentions to take summer classes, work as a resident assistant to cover room and board expenses, and change my major to mathematics.

"Mom, Dad," I said, my voice shaking slightly, "I know I've disappointed you, but I have a plan. I'll make this work. I'm going to dedicate myself to turning this around."

I held my breath, waiting for their response. To my relief, they looked at each other and then back at me with understanding in their eyes.

"We believe in you, David," my mom said, her voice firm but kind. "You can do this. You have our support."

My mother nodded, adding, "We know you can do it. Just remember why you're there and what you're working towards."

Their words filled me with a mix of relief and determination. *I won't let them down again*, I promised myself.

With their backing, I returned to SMU that summer, determined to prove myself. Over the next five semesters, I transformed my academic performance, earning close to a 4.0 GPA over the rest of my time, which clearly reflected my dedication and passion.

Each improved grade felt like a personal victory. *This is for you, Mom and Dad.* I pushed through late-night study sessions and challenging exams with them in mind.

The lessons were profound. I learned the importance of commitment, both in setting goals and following through with action. I realized that with dedication and support, even the most difficult situations can be overcome.

I'm grateful for the commitment my parents showed in believing in me, even during challenging times. Their constant support and my determination led to success, not only for myself but also for my younger brother who followed in our footsteps at SMU.

Years later, when my younger brother was preparing for college, I sat him down and shared my story. "Learn from my journey, it's not about being perfect," I told him. "It's about perseverance and making the most of the opportunities we're given."

This story shows the transformative power of commitment, perseverance, and the belief in one's ability to achieve one's goals. As I look back on those challenging years, I'm filled with gratitude for my family's unwavering support and the valuable lessons I learned about resilience and self-determination.

I picture my parents' faces on that day when I presented my plan. *Thank you. Your belief in me changed everything.*

MASTER TEACHINGS
Commitment illustrated through
Zig Ziglar's Priming the Pump story

Zig Ziglar's teachings on "priming the pump" and the story of the traveler intersect to offer profound insights into achieving success through a commitment to persistence and continuous effort.

I remember the first time I heard Zig Ziglar tell this story. His enthusiastic voice painted a vivid picture in my mind. As I listened, I couldn't help but draw parallels to my own journey in business.

In Zig Ziglar's narrative of "priming the pump," the traveler encounters a farmer with a water pump and learns the importance of priming it with water to draw water from the well. Initially skeptical, the traveler follows the farmer's instructions and begins the process of priming and pumping. However, he soon realizes the pumping is the most challenging part of the task.

"Now, son," Ziglar's voice boomed, imitating the farmer, "you've got to keep pumping. It might seem like nothing's happening at first, but trust me, the water's coming."

As I listened, I thought about my early days in sales. *How many times did I feel like I was pumping with no results? If only I had heard this story then.*

With each pump, the traveler faces resistance and fatigue. Doubts creep in, and he questions whether the effort is worth the reward. The farmer, sensing the traveler's hesitation, offers words of encouragement and reminds him of the abundant water waiting to flow from the well.

"But what if it doesn't work?" the traveler asks, his voice tinged with doubt.

"It will work," the farmer assures him. "You just gotta keep at it. The water's down there, waiting for you to bring it up."

I felt a lump in my throat, remembering times when I was close to giving up. *How many opportunities did I miss because I stopped pumping too soon?*

Despite the challenges, the traveler persists. He continues to prime and pump, pushing through moments of doubt and exhaustion. As he maintains his efforts, he notices incremental progress—the pump becomes easier to operate, and water begins to trickle out, eventually rushing out.

Ziglar's storytelling prowess makes the concept of "priming the pump" not only relatable but also deeply impactful. His ability to weave a compelling narrative with valuable life lessons makes his teachings resonate with audiences seeking motivation and guidance.

"You see," Ziglar says, his voice filled with conviction, "success is like that pump. You've got to prime it with effort, keep pumping even when you don't see results, and trust that the rewards will come."

The traveler's journey mirrors the experiences of individuals striving for their goals. Like the traveler, they encounter obstacles and setbacks along the way. However, by staying committed to the process and putting in the necessary effort, they can overcome challenges and realize their aspirations.

I thought about a recent big goal that was testing my patience. I'd been pumping for weeks with little to show for it. *But maybe, just maybe, I'm on the verge of a breakthrough.*

This narrative underscores the importance of commitment to consistency, determination, and persistence in achieving success. The combination of Zig Ziglar's "priming the pump" story and the traveler's tale emphasizes the power of continuous effort and resilience.

Watching Ziglar's passionate delivery and insightful commentary in his video on "priming the pump" further reinforces these valuable life lessons, inspiring individuals on their journey toward personal and professional growth.

As the video ended, I felt a renewed sense of determination. "Much obliged, Zig," I whispered, feeling as if he was speaking directly to me. "I'm ready to keep pumping, no matter what."

This story has become a touchstone and reminder to persist. Whenever I feel like giving up, I hear Ziglar's voice in my head: *Keep pumping, the water's coming.* And with that, I find the strength to push forward, knowing that success might be just one more pump away.

TRENT TAKEAWAYS

- Stay in the grind long enough.

- Commitment is the fuel that propels you towards your goals, even in challenging times.

- How do setbacks or challenges shape your commitment and determination?

"When you want to succeed as badly as you want to breathe, then you'll be successful."

~Eric Thomas

CHAPTER 9

DISTRESS

ENTREPRENEURIAL INSPIRATION
Embracing Challenges: How Determination, Faith, and Strategic Learning Paved the Way for Entrepreneurial Success

Back to 1996. I took a leap of faith and started Trent Capital Management at 33. With a well-thought-out business strategy and a strong sense of determination, I was ready to conquer the financial industry as a sole owner.

This is it—I thought to myself on the first day, standing in my modest 300 square foot office—*my chance to make a real difference in people's financial lives.*

But soon enough, I faced the tough truths of entrepreneurship, which tested my assumptions and pushed me to overcome unforeseen obstacles.

Within just a few months, I realized my revenue and expense projections were significantly off target. This revelation was a tough pill to swallow, especially when coupled with the realization that I needed to invest more than anticipated in marketing and advertising to attract clients.

I remember sitting at my desk late one night, poring over the numbers, feeling the knot of anxiety in my stomach.

How could I have been so off?

With limited financial resources, I had no choice but to resort to borrowing money, eventually through high-interest credit cards, to sustain the business through its infancy.

As I signed yet another credit card application, I wondered: *Am I making a huge mistake? Should I cut my losses and go back to a steady job?*

I refused to succumb to distress and discouragement. Instead, I doubled down on my determination and resilience, which included a more rigorous routine of incorporating prayers into my daily life, and seeking guidance and strength from a higher power.

Each morning, before starting my day, I closed my eyes and prayed: *Please grant me the wisdom to navigate these challenges and the strength to persevere. Help me to remain steadfast in my vision and to trust in the journey ahead.*

Additionally, I immersed myself in the teachings of esteemed personal development experts like Jim Rohn, Zig Ziglar, Earl Nightingale, and Norman Vincent Peale. Their wisdom guided me during moments of uncertainty and doubt, reminding me that success is built on perseverance and a positive mindset.

I can still hear Zig Ziglar's voice in my head. "You don't have to be great to start, but you have to start to be great." These words became my mantra.

Michael Gerber's groundbreaking book, *The E-Myth* significantly impacted my approach to business providing me with strategic insights and practical strategies for navigating entrepreneurship, such as understanding the importance of working *on* my business rather than just in it.

I've been so caught up in the day-to-day that I've forgotten to look at the big picture and work "on" in addition to "in" my business. Gerber taught me to create systems and processes to streamline operations and enhance client service, addressing issues like inconsistent client acquisition and inefficient workflows.

Being the sole proprietor of my business, I carried the weight of making crucial decisions without external influence. In a scenario with business partners, their advice might've leaned toward considering closure.

There were nights when I lay awake, questioning my decisions. *What if they're right? What if I should just cut my losses?* But then I'd remember why I started this journey in the first place.

However, my steadfast determination and deep belief in the vision of Trent Capital Management propelled me, even when the path seemed uncertain. *I've come too far to give up now. I owe it to my clients and to myself to see this through.*

It wasn't until the fourth year of operations that I began to witness a more favorable balance between revenue and expenses. I remember the day I looked at the books and saw a profit for the first time. Tears welled up in my eyes as I whispered, "We made it. We actually made it."

Over time, I diligently worked toward paying off debts and steered the company toward sustained growth and success. Those early struggles were instrumental in shaping the resilient and resourceful entrepreneur I am today.

As I look back on those challenging early years, I'm filled with a mix of pride and gratitude. *Thank you*, I often think, to the version of myself that refused to give up, to the mentors whose words guided me, and to the faith that sustained me. *Every struggle was a lesson, every setback a learning moment and trajectory waiting to happen.*

Those experiences taught me that entrepreneurship isn't just about having a good idea or a solid business plan. It's about having the grit to weather the storms, the humility to learn from mistakes, and the vision to see beyond immediate events to the potential that lies ahead.

FAMILY VALUES

Transforming Adversity into Strength: How Bullying in 7th Grade Shaped My Resilience and Empathy

It's 7th grade at Central Junior High School, and it's easy to see it as a time filled with distress and trauma. As a typically small and shy kid, I found solace in my close friends but faced a different reality when targeted by a couple of significantly larger kids who subjected me to relentless bullying throughout the year.

Each day in first period felt like a battle against a kid who seemed determined to make my life miserable, resorting to both verbal and occasional physical attacks. I vividly remember one day when he sneered, "What's the matter, Trent? Can't you stand up for yourself?"

I felt a knot tighten in my stomach. *What is going on in his life that made him so cruel?* Perhaps he was dealing with his own pain that I couldn't see.

I walked down the hallway, clutching my books tightly to my chest, when he shoved me hard against the lockers. "You're such a weakling," he spat, his face twisted with anger.

I looked up at him, my heart pounding in my chest. *Why does he hate me so much?* I felt afraid and confused. *What did I ever do to him?*

Despite the challenges, that time played a crucial role in shaping who I am today. It taught me resilience, empathy, and the strength to persevere even in the face of adversity. It was a reminder of my own inner strength and ability to overcome obstacles.

I remember coming home one day, tears streaming down my face. My mother noticed immediately and pulled me into a comforting hug. "What's wrong, David?" she asked gently.

"It's just. . . this kid at school," I stammered. "He's always picking on me. I don't know what to do."

She looked at me with a mix of concern and determination. "David, you are stronger than you think. Don't let him define who you are. Stand tall and remember that you have the power to rise above this."

Maybe she's right, I thought. *Maybe I can find a way to get through this.*

What's remarkable is how those times became a catalyst for personal growth and prosperity. Through adversity, I discovered hidden reserves of strength and resilience within myself that I may not have tapped into otherwise. Challenges, while difficult, can also be transformative and empowering.

I also gained empathy for those who bullied me. I realized their actions were likely rooted in their own struggles, whether at home or elsewhere. This understanding allowed me to let go of any lingering resentment and instead fostered a sense of compassion.

One day, years later, I ran into my old bully at a local store. He looked different, older, and somewhat weary. "Hey, Trent," he said, his voice lacking the malice it once held. "I just wanted to say I'm sorry for how I treated you back then."

I felt a surprising sense of calm. "It's okay," I replied, genuinely meaning it. "We all have our struggles."

Overall, my 7th-grade experience was challenging, but it became a cornerstone of my personal growth journey.

I realize that the pain I endured was not in vain. *I am so grateful to the younger version of myself who endured those hardships. My strength and resilience have shaped the person I am today.*

MASTER TEACHINGS

Success Requires Breathless Determination: The Power of Intense Desire in Achieving Your Aspirations

Once upon a time, there was a young man consumed by an unquenchable thirst for wealth and success. During this pivotal time, he encountered a wise guru who held the key to unlocking the secrets of success. Approaching the guru with fervor and determination, the young man poured out his aspirations.

"I want to achieve the same level of success and wealth as you. Please, reveal to me the secret," he pleaded, his eyes shining with hope and ambition.

As I listened to this story told by Eric Thomas on one of my audio programs for the first time, I saw myself in that young man. *How many times have I felt that burning desire for success?* I thought, remembering my own early struggles.

The guru, with a serene smile, responded, "Meet me at the beach tomorrow at 4 a.m., and I will share with you the secret to success."

Curiosity piqued and anticipation high, the young man arrived at the beach the next morning, ready to absorb the guru's wisdom. Little did he know that what awaited him was not a conventional lesson but a profound revelation.

As the young man stood by the water's edge, the guru beckoned him into the waves. Without explanation, the guru submerged the young man's head underwater, catching him off guard. Panic set in as the young man struggled for breath, the weight of the water pressing down on him like what he faced in his quest for success. In that moment of desperation, all he could think about was the primal need to breathe.

I could almost feel the panic of the young man, remembering times when I felt overwhelmed by building my business. There were moments when I felt like I was drowning in responsibilities.

Just as he felt his strength waning, the guru pulled him back up, gasping for air and reeling from the intensity of the experience. With a calm yet penetrating gaze, the guru asked a simple question, "What did you desire most when your head was underwater?"

Still catching his breath and trying to make sense of the ordeal, the young man replied, "I wanted to breathe!"

It was then that the guru imparted the timeless wisdom that would resonate deeply with the young man throughout his journey. "When you yearn for success as intensely as you yearned for that breath, then and only then will you truly achieve it."

These words struck me. *Is my desire for success that intense? Am I willing to fight for it as if my life depended on it?*

Just like my early days at Trent Capital Management, where every challenge was met with resilience and a relentless pursuit of success, this story parallels my path to achieving my aspirations. I remember sitting in my small office, staring at the mounting bills and thinking, *I need to make this work; my dreams depend on it.*

That feeling of urgency was like the need for air, driving me to push through every obstacle and keep striving for my goals. There were nights I couldn't sleep; my mind raced with ideas and strategies. *Is this what the guru meant? Is this the kind of desire that leads to success?*

I recall a day when our efforts at attaining new clients weren't working. I sat at my desk and felt defeated; the guru's words echoed in my mind. *Do I want this as badly as I want to breathe?*

The answer was a resounding "Yes!" It gave me the strength to collaborate with my team and think and create new strategies for client acquisition. I knew if our team kept taking action, we'd figure it out.

This parable became a reminder to check in with myself regularly. *Am I still hungry for success? Do I still have that breathless determination?* It pushed me to maintain my focus and drive, even when things got tough.

As I share this story with others now, I often see that same spark of recognition in their eyes. "Have you ever wanted something so badly that it felt like you couldn't breathe without it?" I ask them. "That's the level of desire you need to succeed."

This lesson, simple yet profound, shaped my approach to business and life. It's not just about working hard; it's about having an unwavering—almost primal—drive to achieve your goals. It's about wanting success as desperately as you want air when you're under water. . .

TRENT TAKEAWAYS

- Live by the phrase, "Everything in life happens for me, not to me."

- True entrepreneurs are survivors because they simply never quit.

- Ask yourself, how can I view my life as a living laboratory?

"The secret of getting ahead is getting started."

~Mark Twain

CHAPTER 10

BOSS

ENTREPRENEURIAL INSPIRATION
Being my own boss—the true test at
Trent Capital Management

As I continued my entrepreneurial journey with Trent Capital Management, I embraced the role of being the captain of my own ship, navigating the exciting yet turbulent waters of entrepreneurship. The idea of being my own boss conjured up images of freedom, flexibility, and financial success. This idea aligns with those who crave independence and the ability to steer their own professional path.

I remember deciding to start Trent Capital Management. I sat in my living room, contemplating the leap. *This is it, David. No more safety net. It's all on you now.* I was afraid and excited.

My journey as a boss began when I dove into the world of sales at the age of 24, kickstarting my career at New York Life on a commission-only basis. Even though I had a sales manager to answer to, the spirit of independence already thrived within me.

I recall my first day at New York Life, nervously straightening my tie before walking into the office. *You've got this. This is your first step towards true independence.*

While I did relish the perks of entrepreneurship, the reality was far from a bed of roses. Being your own boss entails wearing multiple hats, from CEO to janitor, especially in the early days of building a business.

One day, I prepared for an important client meeting when I noticed the office bathroom needed cleaning. As I scrubbed the toilet, I laughed at the irony. *From financial advisor to janitor in the span of five minutes, this is what being your own boss really means.*

I vividly recall the humorous realization of the additional expenses that came with my newfound freedom, like the 8% FICA contribution I had to match for myself as both employer and employee—a classic "ouch" moment.

When I saw that first payroll statement, my eyes widened in disbelief. "Wait, I have to pay both parts of FICA?" I exclaimed to my empty office. "Nobody told me about this part of being the boss!"

"The buck stops here" epitomizes the weight of responsibility that rests on entrepreneurs' shoulders. It signifies taking ownership of decisions, successes, and failures alike without the luxury of passing the blame.

We had one tough quarter when we missed our revenue targets. As I sat alone in my office early one morning, pouring over the numbers, the weight of responsibility crushed me. *There's no one else to blame. It's all on me to turn this around.*

When mentoring aspiring entrepreneurs, I often emphasize the trade-offs that come with the territory. This path is paved with moments of loneliness, stress, and relentless accountability, yet it's also filled with unparalleled rewards and a sense of accomplishment that transcends the ordinary.

During a recent mentoring session, a young entrepreneur asked me, "Is it worth it? All the stress and responsibility?"

I paused, thinking back. "It's not easy. There will be days when you question everything. But when you see your vision come to life, when you create jobs and make a difference in people's lives—that feeling is unmatched."

Being an entrepreneur is like conducting a grand orchestra of ups and downs, a quest for self-awareness, strength, and relentless drive. It requires bravery, flexibility, and a burning desire to pave your own way, understanding that each obstacle and victory molds the mark you make on the world.

I often think about that nervous 24-year-old starting out at New York Life. *If only you knew what was ahead, the challenges, the triumphs, the lessons—it's all part of the beautiful chaos of being your own boss.*

The path of entrepreneurship is not for everyone, but for those who embrace it, it's a journey of self-discovery and impact. It's about creating something from nothing, about leaving your mark on the world. And despite the challenges, I wouldn't have it any other way.

FAMILY VALUES
Embracing the Bossman Mentality:
The Power of Mentorship and Connection

In the vibrant commotion of parenthood, I had a delightful encounter with my son, Carter, a spirited soul even at the tender age of four. It was one of those typical moments where parental directives collided with youthful independence.

"Carter, it's time to clean up your toys," I said, trying to keep my voice firm but gentle.

His little face scrunched up in defiance, and in a playful tone, Carter boldly proclaimed, "You're not the boss of me!"

His animated tone and determined gaze were enough to make me hold back a chuckle. *Oh, the irony of parenting. One day they're declaring independence, the next they're asking for help tying their shoes,* I thought.

With a gentle smile, I reminded him, "Actually, buddy, I *am* the boss of you. But let's be a team and clean up together, okay?"

I helped him pick up his toys and marveled at his budding independence. *Where does the time go? It feels like just yesterday he was learning to walk, and now he's asserting his autonomy.*

Fast forward to Carter's college days at Trinity College in Hartford, Connecticut, where he played on the basketball team alongside his good friend and teammate, Eric Dean. Eric, in his affable manner, started calling me "Bossman."

The first time I heard it, I was taken aback. *Bossman?* I thought, amused. *Is that how the kids see me now?*

The nickname stuck and continues to be his favored term of endearment, even as he navigates his early 30s. It never fails to bring a smile to my face whenever I receive a text from him that begins with "Bossman."

Every time I see that word pop up on my phone, I'm transported back to those college basketball games, cheering from the stands. *From 'you're not the boss of me' to 'Bossman.' Life has a funny way of coming full circle.*

The saga of "Bossman" took an unexpected turn in 2021 when I mentored our new hire John Sidery, a bright and ambitious young 29-year-old Certified Financial Planner. In our interactions, John quickly adopted the habit of addressing me as "Bossman" as well, without any prior knowledge of Eric's endearing nickname.

During one of our mentoring sessions, John casually dropped the term. "So, Bossman, what do you think about this investment strategy?"

I paused, struck by the coincidence. *Is this some kind of cosmic joke?* I grinned.

It was as if the Universe conspired to bestow upon me this honorary title.

Intrigued by the term's significance, I stumbled upon an interesting definition of "Bossman" in Caribbean English, where it signifies entrepreneurship or ownership in a small business. It dawned on me that beyond its playful charm, "Bossman" carried an essence of respect and admiration, reflecting the bonds forged through mentorship and camaraderie.

As I pondered this, a warmth spread through my chest. *It's not just a nickname*, I realized. *It's a symbol of the relationships I've built, the trust I've earned.*

Reflecting on these whimsical encounters, I pondered the idea of adopting "Bossman" as more than just a nickname. While I cherish the sentiment behind it, I also recognize the humility and camaraderie it embodies, making it a badge of honor in the journey of mentorship and friendship.

From being the 'boss' of a defiant four-year-old to being called 'Bossman' by those I mentor. I shook my head in amazement. *Life has a beautiful way of evolving our roles and relationships.*

As I sit in my office, surrounded by mementos of my journey—from family photos to business accolades—I can't help but feel grateful for these connections. *Bossman: It's not about authority or power. It's about guidance, support, and mutual respect.*

This realization deepened my commitment to mentorship and fostering meaningful connections. Whether it's with my children, mentees, or colleagues, I strive to embody the true spirit of "Bossman," not as a ruler, but as a guide and friend on this shared journey of growth and success.

MASTER TEACHINGS
Bossing Myself Around: The Key to Self-Discipline and Entrepreneurial Success

During my quest for impactful reads, I stumbled upon a hidden gem in 2018 that left a mark on me: Darren Hardy's *The Entrepreneur Roller Coaster,* which hit the shelves in 2015. I flipped through the pages, and felt a surge of excitement. *This is exactly what I've been looking for!*

Despite being a recent addition to my reading list compared to timeless classics, this book swiftly became a favorite and a trusted resource. What really resonated with me was how Hardy's mentorship under the legendary Jim Rohn, a titan in personal development, shone through his words and deeply connected with me.

I remember sitting in my office when a particular passage caught my eye. Hardy wrote, "The most successful people in the world have one thing in common: they boss themselves around." It was like a lightbulb moment. *Is this what I've been missing?*

I summarized that standout lesson from Hardy's book in the phrase "boss myself around," which I've shortened to BMA. It all boils down to self-discipline, self-motivation, and self-accountability—the fundamental pillars of successful entrepreneurship and effective life management.

I remembered all the times I waited for external motivation or guidance. *How much time have I wasted waiting for someone or something else to push me?* I felt a mix of regret and determination.

The notion of "bossing myself around" revolves around taking full ownership of my actions, decisions, and productivity, much like how a boss leads their team. Instead of waiting for external motivation or guidance, this approach empowers individuals to set clear objectives, craft actionable plans, and hold themselves accountable for their progress. They must answer to themselves.

I recall the first time I consciously applied this principle. It was a Monday morning, and I had to prepare for a daunting client meeting. Instead of procrastinating, I looked in the mirror and said, "Alright, David. It's time to get to work. No excuses." It felt a bit silly at first, but the impact was immediate.

Embracing this shift in mindset significantly boosted my efficiency and output. It's all about being proactive, staying laser-focused on priorities, conquering procrastination, and confronting life head-on with grit and resilience.

There were days I struggled to maintain this self-discipline. I remember one day when I was tempted to put off an important but difficult task. *Come on, boss,* (channeling Hardy's teachings) *this needs to get done, and you're the one who has to do it.*

While I may not always execute it flawlessly, adopting the BMA philosophy resulted in numerous triumphs and personal development.

Hardy's emphasis on self-leadership and self-management strikes a chord because it embodies the essence of seizing control of one's own destiny. By bossing ourselves around, we morph into the architects of our success journey, propelling ourselves toward our entrepreneurial dreams and life objectives with unyielding determination and clarity of purpose.

I remember a conversation I had with a mentee who was struggling with self-motivation. "How do you stay so disciplined?" he asked me.

I smiled, remembering my own journey. "I've learned to be my own boss," I replied. "Every morning, I look in the mirror and give myself marching orders for the day. It's not always easy, but it's always worth it."

The concept of BMA has become more than just a strategy for me; it's a way of life. It reminds me daily that the power to achieve my goals lies within. As I continue to boss myself around, I'm not just building a successful business, I'm building a stronger, more disciplined version of myself.

TRENT TAKEAWAYS

- Balancing freedom and responsibility are keys to thriving as an entrepreneur.

- GSD–Get Stuff Done.

- Embrace the "Boss myself around" philosophy in my life for greater success and fulfillment.

"Yet I will not fail, as the others, for in my hands I now hold the charts, which will guide me through perilous waters to shores, which only yesterday seemed but a dream."

~Og Mandino

CHAPTER 11

BOOKS

ENTREPRENEURIAL INSPIRATION

Empowering Potential: How Mentorship and Belief in One Another Can Transform Lives and Inspire Success

One of the most fulfilling stories of my entrepreneurial journey involves my friendship with Marlon Haynes. Marlon, who was 21 at the time, crossed paths with me when I was 36. It was during the early years of establishing Trent Capital Management in 1996, and I sensed some promising momentum building.

I remember thinking: *We're finally gaining traction. But there's still so much to learn, so much to do.*

Marlon had college experience but dropped out and sold lunches in our building. He worked for a company that went from office to office, offering sandwiches to those who preferred to buy from his company instead of going out. It was through a conversation with my assistant that Marlon's passion for basketball came to light. Knowing my son Carter and I shared the same passion, she introduced Marlon to me.

As we sat down for our initial conversation, Marlon noticed the numerous bookshelves filled with books in my office. His eyes widened as he scanned the shelves. "What's up with all these books?" he asked.

I smiled, feeling a surge of enthusiasm. "These books have been pivotal for my career. They helped me learn life and business lessons that've shaped my success since I was 24," I replied, running my hand along the spines of some of my favorites.

As I spoke, I thought: *If I had someone to guide me to these books when I was his age, it would've really helped me.*

This conversation sparked a serious reading habit in Marlon. This encounter marked the beginning of an incredible journey and relationship between Marlon, my son Carter, and myself. Marlon, being a basketball instructor and trainer, started mentoring my son while I offered him guidance and personal development whenever he sought it.

I remember the first time I saw Marlon working with Carter on the basketball court. The patience and passion he showed reminded me of the mentors who guided me. *Here's how we give back to others*! I felt pride and gratitude.

Marlon once shared, "David was the first person to instill in me that I could set goals and succeed. Growing up, I was taught to see myself as a victim because of my race, but he showed me that I had the power to change my narrative."

His words hit me hard. *How many others are out there, full of potential, just waiting for someone to believe in them?*

Today, Marlon often attributes our relationship as one of the key factors contributing to his success. He has had a remarkable impact on my son Carter as well, and that relationship continues to this day. Carter is 33 now.

Carter also acknowledges Marlon's influence, stating, "Marlon taught me not just about basketball but about life. His mentorship helped shape who I am today, and I take those lessons with me."

Hearing Carter speak about Marlon's impact always fills me with a mix of emotions—pride in both of them, gratitude for the unexpected connections life brings, and a renewed sense of purpose in mentoring others.

What's truly remarkable is that Marlon embarked on his own entrepreneurial journey with a commercial janitorial company called 21st Century Janitorial in 2001. Since then, his enterprise has grown immensely under his leadership. It continues to thrive, and I have no doubt it will expand in the future.

I remember the day Marlon told me about his business idea. "David, I'm thinking of starting my own janitorial company."

"That's fantastic, Marlon! What's your plan?"

This is it. This is why we mentor, why we share our knowledge. To see others take flight.

Watching Marlon's journey from selling sandwiches to starting and running a successful business has been one of the most rewarding experiences of my career. It's a powerful reminder of the ripple effect that mentorship and belief can have.

I'm struck now by how a simple conversation about books led to such a profound and lasting connection. There's a power in sharing knowledge, believing in others, and in the transformative impact of mentorship.

We never know how far our influence will reach. Every interaction, every piece of advice, every show of faith in someone's potential—it all matters.

This experience with Marlon and Carter deepened my commitment to mentorship. Entrepreneurship isn't just about building businesses, but about building people and relationships that can change lives.

FAMILY VALUES

Transformative Wisdom: How the Power of Positive Thinking Sparks Renewal and Purpose in Our Lives

Books have shaped my beliefs and influenced my journey in profound ways. One particular book, *The Power of Positive Thinking* by Norman Vincent Peale, holds a special place in my heart and led to remarkable transformations in the lives of those I've shared it with.

I remember the first time I read it, feeling a surge of hope and possibility. *This is it. This is the mindset that can change everything!*

My passion for sharing the wisdom of books extended beyond my personal life and into my professional practices. Early in my days at Trent Capital Management, I came up with the idea to begin sending clients a book on their birthday every year. As my client base grew, this became more of a challenge, but I was determined to keep it up.

I recently did the math and realized I've sent over 3000 books to clients on their birthdays. Each book was a carefully chosen piece of wisdom, a way to connect with my clients on a deeper level and share something that could potentially change their lives.

Ryan Woolard, my nephew, was grappling with negativity and a sense of being lost. In a moment that felt divinely guided, he stumbled upon a song, *Reset* by OutKast, which spoke directly to his soul, reminding him that everything happens for a reason and urging him to start anew.

That same day, Ryan's path intersected with mine when he visited my office and noticed the book *The Power of Positive Thinking* in my collection. His eyes lingered on the spine, and he asked, "What's that book about?"

This might be the pivotal moment for Ryan! I couldn't resist sharing the book's wisdom with him.

"It's about transforming your life through the power of positive thinking," I explained, pulling the book from the shelf. "It's helped me through some of my toughest times."

It had a profound impact on his life. As Ryan delved into the book, he embarked on a journey of self-discovery and renewal. He prayed for release, sought counseling, and experienced a transformative reset.

Weeks later, Ryan came back to my office, his eyes shining. "Uncle David," he said, his voice filled with emotion, "this book—it's changed everything!"

I felt a lump in my throat, overwhelmed by the change I saw in him. *This is why we share wisdom. This is how we help each other grow.*

The positive changes in Ryan were palpable, radiated outward, and caught the attention of those around him. His newfound clarity and purpose sparked a desire to lead others to hope and love, igniting a passion for ministry.

Fast-forward to a serendipitous lunch encounter a short time later, where a simple question from Wayne Johnson, a deacon from Calvary Baptist Church, unlocked Ryan's calling. "What do you see yourself doing in the future?" Wayne asked.

With staunch conviction, Ryan expressed, "I want to help people find hope and purpose, maybe even as a pastor."

Wayne's eyes lit up. "Of course you can!" he exclaimed. "You have the heart for it. Just take that first step."

As I heard about this conversation later, I marveled at the chain of events. *From a book on my shelf to a life-changing conversation. We never know how far our influence will reach.*

This set in motion a series of events that profoundly shaped his future.

Ryan's journey didn't stop there. Immersed in Chinese culture, he found a deep connection that eventually led him to meet his wife, Lily. Today, Ryan, now 38, serves as a pastor in a Chinese church in New Jersey, living out his calling and impacting countless lives.

I remember the day Ryan called to tell me about his new role. "Uncle David," he said, his voice filled with joy, "I'm living my purpose. And it all started with that book you shared."

I know in my heart that my mom is looking down from heaven and is so proud that Ryan is a minister. Her love for faith and family continues to inspire us all.

Ryan's story shows the power of positivity, faith, and the profound impact of sharing wisdom through books. It's a reminder that even in our darkest moments, there's always a path to renewal and purpose.

"David showed me that I could set goals and succeed. His belief in me changed my life," Ryan said.

Hearing these words always fills me with a mix of humility and gratitude. *We're all just passing on the wisdom we've received, and in doing so, we're changing lives, one book at a time.*

This experience deepened my commitment to sharing knowledge and wisdom. It's reinforced my belief in the power of positive thinking and the transformative impact of books. Every time I look at my bookshelf now, I don't just see books, but potential catalysts for change and growth.

Who else might need this wisdom? Whose life might be transformed by the right book at the right time?

It's a powerful reminder that our actions, even something as simple as sharing a book, can have far-reaching consequences. We never know how a single act of kindness or shared wisdom might ripple out, touching lives in ways we could never imagine.

MASTER TEACHINGS
Unlocking Growth: How Every Moment in Transit Can Transform into an Opportunity for Learning and Self-Improvement

Embarking on a journey, whether on the open road or in the daily rhythms of life, presents a unique opportunity for growth and learning. Zig Ziglar famously coined the term "Automobile University," recognizing the potential of utilizing time spent in the car for personal development.

This concept resonated so deeply I once proudly displayed "AUTO U" on my license plate, a constant reminder of the value I place on continuous learning.

I remember when I decided to get that license plate and filled out the application. *This will be my daily reminder to never waste a moment.* Every time I got into my car I felt a sense of purpose. *What can I learn today?* I was eager to press play on the latest audiobook or podcast.

A study conducted by the University of Southern California found that if you live in a metropolitan area and drive 12,000 miles a year, you can gain the equivalent of two years of college education in just three years by listening to educational content in your car. Considering that the average American adult spends anywhere from 200 to 700 hours per year in a vehicle, this is encouraging news!

I often share this study with friends and colleagues. "Did you know you could earn the equivalent of a college degree just by listening to audiobooks during your commute?" I say, watching eyes widen in surprise. "Imagine what you could achieve with all that knowledge!"

The "Auto U" concept extends beyond driving; it encompasses any activity where we engage our minds while completing routine tasks. Audiobooks and podcasts can transform routine activities into growth opportunities. Even while shaving or preparing a meal, I immerse myself in audiobooks or podcasts, usually on leadership or personal development, continually expanding my horizons.

One morning I caught an insightful segment from a leadership audiobook while I shaved. *Wow, that's a game-changer* and jotted down notes with one hand while holding the razor in the other. *I need to implement this strategy today.*

Walking and strength training sessions become more than physical exercises; they become mental workouts. I tune into podcasts covering a range of topics from entrepreneurship to mindfulness. Each step or lift is accompanied by valuable insights and perspectives shared by experts and thought leaders.

In one workout session where I felt like giving up, a podcast episode on resilience and grit came on. "You can do this," the speaker said, as if speaking directly to me. "Push through the pain, and you'll come out stronger on the other side." Those words fueled my determination, and I finished the workout with renewed energy.

The versatility of "Auto U" lies in its adaptability to various situations. It's not just about filling idle time but about actively seeking knowledge and wisdom in every moment available. Whether in transit or engaged in daily tasks, the habit of continuous learning fuels personal growth.

Zig Ziglar's wisdom reminds us that we're never limited by our circumstances; instead, we can use every moment as an opportunity to invest in ourselves. "Auto U" is not just a concept; it's a mindset—an intentional choice to make the most of our time and unlock our full potential, one podcast episode or audiobook chapter at a time.

I recall a conversation with a young entrepreneur who struggled to find time for personal development. "I just don't have the time," he lamented.

"Do you drive to work?" I asked.

"Yes, about 30 minutes each way," he replied.

"That's an hour a day you could be learning," I said, smiling. "Welcome to Auto U."

As I reflect on my own journey, I realize how much I've grown thanks to this mindset. *Every moment is an opportunity*, I remind myself daily. *What will you learn today?*

This approach has not only enriched my knowledge but has also inspired those around me to embrace continuous learning. It's a powerful reminder that we have the power to transform even the most mundane moments into opportunities for growth and self-improvement.

TRENT TAKEAWAYS

- AUTO U–Enroll in Automobile University.

- Readers are leaders.

- The book you don't read won't help you.

"The most powerful leadership tool you have is your own example."

~John Wooden

CHAPTER 12

ENERGY

ENTREPRENEURIAL INSPIRATION
Embracing Energy and Compassion:
Lessons from a Lifelong Friendship

Lance Bozman was more than just a friend; he was a powerhouse of energy wrapped in Southern charm and authentic excitement. We first met during our college days at SMU, where we both joined the same fraternity, Alpha Tau Omega. Although we were buddies back then, it wasn't until our late twenties that our friendship truly blossomed.

I remember the day we reconnected after college. As Lance walked into the room, I thought: *How does he still have so much energy? It's like he never left campus.*

What made Lance truly special was his infectious enthusiasm and knack for brightening up any room and making everyone feel at home. When we first met, he proudly proclaimed in his Texan accent, "I'm from the big I in the sky, Irving, Texas; the nucleus of the world."

I chuckled. *The nucleus of the world? Really, Lance?* I was amused by his bold claim.

It was a nod to his hometown, Irving, and a tribute to Ross Perot's famous quote about Irving being the center of his business universe at EDS. To this day, I still wonder if Lance intentionally mispronounced nucleus as "nuchlalas."

"Lance," I once asked him, "do you really mean to say 'nuchlalas' instead of 'nucleus'?"

He grinned, that mischievous twinkle in his eye. "Now, David, where's the fun in being correct all the time?"

But beyond the catchy phrases and larger-than-life personality, what truly made Lance stand out was his genuine concern for others. Whenever we talked, he delved deep into how I was doing, how my family was, and how my business was going. He had a way of making you feel valued, important, and supported.

During one of our catch-up sessions, Lance asked, "David, how's that new venture of yours coming along? Any challenges I can help with?"

I was taken aback by his sincere interest. *Why does he care so much?* I wondered. *Most people just ask out of politeness.*

Lance wasn't just a client; he was a mentor. His dedication to caring for others and making a real impact in their lives influenced how I interacted with both my team and our clients. I learned from him the significance of not only conducting business but also forming meaningful relationships based on trust and genuine care.

Frustrated one day, I thought: *What would Lance do in this situation?* It was then I realized how much his approach influenced my leadership style.

Interestingly, Lance (in his thirties) also ventured into entrepreneurship through commercial real estate in Europe and relocated to Budapest, Hungary, where he achieved wonderful success before eventually returning to the US after exiting his company. I've always found it fascinating that he followed a similar path to mine.

When I heard about his success in Budapest, I felt a mix of admiration and curiosity. *How did he make such a big leap? And how can I channel some of that courage in my own ventures?*

One day, I asked him about his decision to move to Budapest. "Lance, what made you take such a big risk?"

He laughed, that booming laugh that filled the room. "Dude, sometimes you've got to jump off the cliff and build your wings on the way down."

I'm so grateful for the lessons Lance taught me, not through lectures, but his actions and unwavering support. His energy, genuine care for others, and fearless approach to entrepreneurship continue to inspire me.

I'm grateful to Lance for showing me that success in business and life is about more than just profits; it's about the energy and care you bring to every interaction.

He also taught me the power of genuine connections, the importance of bringing positive energy to every situation, and the courage to take bold steps in pursuit of our dreams. These lessons continue to shape my approach to business and life, reminding me that true success is measured not just in financial terms, but in the lives we touch and the positive energy we spread along the way.

FAMILY VALUES
The Power of Connection:
How Family Bonds Shape Our Journey

"Wait, your brother Steve is in ATO with my brother Blake?" I asked Lance.

"Small world, isn't it?" Lance replied with a grin.

When I realized that Lance and I each had a younger brother who each attended Southern Methodist University (SMU) at the same time and even joined Alpha Tau Omega (ATO) fraternity together, I was in awe, especially since I'd lost touch with Lance since our college days.

How incredible is this? It's like our families are destined to be connected.

The fact that Blake and Steve formed a connection was nothing short of extraordinary. It felt as if fate intervened, blessing us with this unexpected bond.

What's even more astonishing is how Blake and Steve carved their own path in the business world after college. With a few partners, and in their late twenties, they fearlessly delved into the realm of sub-prime lending, providing opportunities for consumers with high credit risks to finance automobiles.

When I heard about their venture, I remember feeling pride and concern. *Sub-prime lending? That's a risky business. But isn't that what entrepreneurship is all about? Taking calculated risks?*

This bold move paid off, leading to a successful exit from their company in their mid-thirties. Their determination and entrepreneurial spirit were truly commendable.

"Blake," I asked one day, "weren't you scared of taking on such a risky venture?"

He looked at me with a confident smile. "Of course I was. But Steve and I believed in what we were doing. Sometimes you have to take the leap."

His words reminded me of my own entrepreneurial journey.

Furthermore, I had the privilege of getting to know the rest of the remarkable Bozman family—Bob, Sandy, and their sister Holly. They were truly exceptional individuals, embodying the same sense of unity and accomplishment my own family cherished.

As I spent time with the Bozmans, I drew parallels to my own family. *It's amazing how similar our families are in values and spirit.*

It served as a poignant reminder of the profound impact strong familial connections can have on shaping our lives.

As adults, my father fondly referred to our family of six as 'The House of Champions,' and when I shared this with the Bozman family, they wholeheartedly embraced the idea, likening their family of five to ours.

I remember sharing this with Lance. "You know, Lance, my dad calls our family the House of Champions," I said, feeling a bit self-conscious.

Lance's face lit up. "I love that! We're like that too, just one champion short," he joked.

His reaction warmed my heart, reinforcing the connection between our families.

Lance and his family shaped my entrepreneurial journey and life perspective by emphasizing passion, compassion, and meaningful connections beyond transactions—embodying true champions.

One day, as Lance and I discussed business strategies, he said something that stuck with me: "Dude, remember, it's not just about the deals. It's about the people you meet and the lives you touch along the way." I nodded.

This is what sets the Bozmans apart. They understand that business is about more than just profits.

I'm forever grateful for their impactful role on my journey.

How fortunate am I, to have not just my own family, but the Bozmans as well, to guide and inspire me?

MASTER TEACHINGS
Timeless Wisdom from John Wooden:
Lessons in Energy and Personal Growth

John Wooden, the basketball coach renowned for his wisdom and leadership, isn't just an author but a beacon of timeless lessons that have shaped countless lives. His teachings (epitomized in the revered *Pyramid of Success*), hold profound wisdom that extends beyond the court into the realm of personal growth and energy management. As someone who has delved deep into Wooden's insights, I can attest to their transformative power.

I remember the first time I picked up Wooden's book. *Can these principles really apply to my life?*

Below are four pivotal lessons from my experiences, intertwined with John Wooden's profound wisdom, particularly focusing on their impact on energy and the importance of energy management.

LESSON 1: GENUINE CARE FOR OTHERS

Wooden emphasized the significance of authentic care for others, going beyond superficial interactions. This depth of concern is not just about social interactions but also about the energy we invest in understanding and supporting others' well-being.

I recall a conversation with Lance Bozman, who embodied this lesson perfectly. "David, how's your family doing?" he asked.

Why does he care so much? I felt surprised and touched.

Such authentic connections not only nurture relationships but also fuel positive energy exchanges. Lance's heartfelt discussions about family reminded me of Wooden's teachings on the importance of caring deeply for others.

LESSON 2: THE IMPACT OF ENTHUSIASM

Wooden believed in the power of enthusiasm to drive motivation and inspiration. Enthusiasm is like a renewable energy source that fuels our actions and attitudes.

Lance's contagious energy and passion for life mirror Wooden's belief in the transformative influence of facing challenges with zest and optimism. I remember a tough day at work when Lance called me.

"David, don't let this get you down," he said, his voice brimming with enthusiasm. "Remember, every challenge is an opportunity in disguise."

His words resonated with me, replenishing my energy reserves and reminding me to approach life with a positive attitude.

LESSON 3: BUILDING MEANINGFUL CONNECTIONS

Wooden emphasized the importance of nurturing genuine and meaningful relationships. Quality connections, rooted in trust and genuine care, contribute significantly to our emotional well-being and energy levels.

Lance's dedication to forming deep connections matches Wooden's philosophy. I remember when I felt overwhelmed.

"Lance, I don't know how to balance everything," I confided.

"David, take a step back and focus on the relationships that matter," he advised. "Those connections will give you the strength to handle anything."

His words reminded me of Wooden's teachings on the energy-enhancing effects of meaningful interactions.

LESSON 4: EMBRACING GRATITUDE ON SHARED PATHS

Wooden taught the value of gratitude and humility in our shared journeys. Recognizing and appreciating the positive influences of individuals like Lance and the Bozman family enriches our experiences and fuels a sense of gratitude, uplifting our energy and outlook on life's paths.

One day, I shared this with Lance. "Lance, I just want to say thank you for everything. Your support means the world to me."

He smiled warmly. "Dude, it's a two-way street. You've been there for me too."

In essence, integrating these lessons into our lives not only enhances our personal growth but also optimizes our energy management. Just as Wooden's teachings have stood the test of time, they continue to illuminate the path toward a more energized and fulfilling existence.

The impact of Lance and the Bozman family on shaping personal and professional journeys aligns well with Wooden's philosophy of recognizing and cherishing meaningful influences.

TRENT TAKEAWAYS

- Acknowledge the deep influence of strong family ties on shaping life paths.

- Be a mentor to others, sharing wisdom and guidance to make a real impact in their lives.

- GCM–Genuine Care and Mentorship.

ESTABLISHING SUCCESS

MY 40s AND 50s AT
TRENT CAPITAL MANAGEMENT–
INNOVATING AND
INVESTING IN OTHERS

"Success begins with a vision, fueled by belief,
and realized through relentless action."

~David Trent

CHAPTER 13

CONCEIVE

ENTREPRENEURIAL INSPIRATION

Conceive, Believe, Achieve: Harnessing the
Power of Vision and Commitment
to Fuel Entrepreneurial Success

Earl Nightingale's wisdom from *Lead the Field* and his profound teaching, "What the mind can conceive and believe, it can achieve," is the essence of personal achievement and success. I like to call it CBA (Conceive, Believe, Achieve).

In 2004, I felt the entrepreneurial fire burning, which led me to establish Absolute Athlete. The inspiration behind this venture stemmed from my son, Carter, who loved basketball from a young age and dreamt of playing at the college level. With the help of skilled basketball trainer Marlon Haynes and strength trainer David Wood, we were fortunate to have the right resources to support Carter's journey.

I remember sitting down with Carter one evening, watching him practice his free throws. "Dad," he said, pausing to catch his breath, "I really want to play college basketball. Do you think I can do it?"

I looked into his determined eyes. "Absolutely, Carter," I replied. "If you conceive it and believe in it, you can achieve it. Let's make it happen."

Carter's dedication to basketball inspired me to create Absolute Athlete, a company centered on "Disciplined Training for Sports and Life." The incorporation of wisdom sessions underscored our commitment to holistic growth, embodying part of the essence of the CBA process.

As we brainstormed ideas, Marlon turned to me and said, "David, this isn't just about training athletes. It's about shaping their lives, giving them the tools to succeed both on and off the court."

I nodded, feeling the weight of his words. "You're right, Marlon. We have a chance to make a real difference here."

The inception of Trent Capital Management in 1996 was also a CBA moment. I often jest about how I was simultaneously naive and overconfident. However, beneath the humor lay a deep commitment to CBA. I meticulously crafted a clear vision and developed a business plan I wholeheartedly believed in.

I recall the day I decided to start Trent Capital Management sitting at my kitchen table, surrounded by drafts of my business plan.

This is it. This is my chance to create something meaningful.

The excitement was palpable, but so was the fear. *What if I fail?* But then I remembered Nightingale's words and pushed forward.

I embraced the confidence needed to take decisive actions toward success. Despite the initial lack of clients and financial instability, and the daunting realization that entrepreneurship required more time and effort than I anticipated, I remained resolute and persevered.

One month, I stared at a nearly empty client list. *How am I going to make this work?* The weight of doubt pressed down on me. But then I remembered the CBA principle.

You've conceived this vision, David. Now believe in it and take action.

The first four to five years were particularly grueling due to market fluctuations and the steep learning curve I faced, yet they laid the foundation for a remarkable 27-year journey.

I often think back to those early days, the sleepless nights and relentless hustle. *Every challenge was a lesson,* I remind myself. *Every setback was a setup for a comeback.*

The CBA principle evolved from a theoretical concept to a practical reality that shapes my decisions, actions, and accomplishments. It continues to guide me forward, driving me toward my objectives and motivating me to achieve greater success in business and personal growth.

Greater success now looks like expanding my influence through Trent Premier Growth, a holistic coaching and consulting service for entrepreneurs and their teams, where I can share the lessons learned and empower others to reach their potential.

As I sit here in my office, I feel so fulfilled.

Every challenge faced and every lesson learned has prepared me for this next chapter. I'm ready to inspire others to believe in their own potential as fiercely as I believe in mine.

I realize that the CBA principle is not just about achieving business success. It's about personal growth, resilience, and the unwavering belief in one's ability to shape their destiny. And as I look to the future, I'm excited to see how many more lives can be transformed through the power of Conceive, Believe, Achieve.

FAMILY VALUES

From Dream to Flight:
How Vision, Belief, and Mentorship
Propel Us Toward Our Aspirations

It was a crisp morning as Carter, and I embarked on a journey from Little Rock to Dallas on a Cessna 414, graciously lent to us by a friend.

Since I'm not a pilot, we had a professional pilot flying the plane, which allowed me to focus on the breathtaking beauty of the world below. As we soared through the skies, surrounded by the vast expanse of clouds, a seed was planted in my mind—*Maybe I'll own a plane like this one day!*

I turned to Carter, who gazed out the window with wide eyes. "Isn't this amazing?" I asked.

"Yeah, Dad," he replied, his voice filled with wonder. "Do you think we could ever have a plane like this?"

His question lingered in my mind.

Why not? If we can dream it, we can achieve it.

The initial conception of airplane ownership seemed daunting, almost unreachable, given the complexities and costs involved. Yet, fueled by the belief that took root in my mind, I held onto that vision tenaciously. I immersed myself in images of flying, envisioning the freedom and exhilaration owning an aircraft would bring.

Gradually, my faith in making this a reality grew stronger, but I also recognized the need for consistent effort. I estimated that purchasing and maintaining an aircraft like the Cessna 414 would require a significant financial commitment—potentially upwards of $700,000, including acquisition costs, insurance, and ongoing maintenance.

As I approached my early 40s, I purchased my first aircraft, a Cessna 414. However, this was just the beginning. With the guidance and mentorship of my friend Greg Hatcher—not only a mentor in business but also an expert in aircraft ownership—I navigated the nuances of owning and operating a plane.

"Be careful, David," Greg cautioned me during one of our discussions. "You're going to feel addicted to this and want something bigger and better."

His words resonated with me, foreshadowing the journey ahead. *Is he right? Will this become a passion that drives me to new heights?*

True to his words, as years went by, I eyed and eventually bought a Cessna 441 Conquest—a significant leap in both capabilities and costs. Through the CBA (Conceive, Believe, Achieve) process once again, I eventually upgraded to a light jet, a Citation 5. It was a milestone in my aviation journey.

I remember the day I took delivery of the Citation 5. Standing on the tarmac, I felt proud and some disbelief.

This is real! I've turned a dream into reality!

The experiences and memories created through these aircraft are nothing short of extraordinary—family trips to scenic destinations, entertaining friends and loved ones at sporting events, and being part of cherished milestones like flying to my pilot Walt's wedding.

One particular trip stands out in my memory. As we flew to a family reunion, Carter turned to me and said, "Dad, this is incredible. Thank you for making this happen."

I smiled, feeling a deep sense of fulfillment. "It's all about believing in our dreams and working hard to achieve them," I replied.

Each flight isn't just a physical journey but proof of the power of the mind and belief in turning dreams into reality. Earl Nightingale continues to echo in my heart, reminding me that with a clear vision, resolute belief, and determined action, the skies of possibility are limitless.

If I can turn this dream into reality, what else am I capable of achieving?

What's next?

What other dreams can I bring to life?

The journey from dream to flight taught me that with vision, belief, and the right mentorship, we can achieve anything we set our minds to. It's a lesson I use every day, inspiring me to reach for the stars and encouraging others to do the same.

MASTER TEACHINGS
What the mind can conceive and believe it can achieve

The *Lead the Field* audio program greatly impacted my 20s and 30s. It remains a favorite. His teaching, "What the mind can conceive and believe, it can achieve," was profound and defines personal achievement.

I drove to work one day feeling stuck in my career, when Nightingale's voice came through my car speakers: "What the mind can conceive and believe, it can achieve." I felt a jolt of electricity run through me.

Could it really be that simple?

Nightingale's teachings emphasize the power of the mind in shaping reality. He suggests that our thoughts and beliefs are the primary drivers of our actions and outcomes. When we conceive a clear and compelling vision in our minds and truly believe in its possibility, we can achieve extraordinary results.

"Your world is a living expression of how you are using and have used your mind," Nightingale's voice continued in my head as I reflected on my own life.

What kind of world have I created with my thoughts?

The first part of Nightingale's teaching, "What the mind can conceive," speaks to the importance of having a clear and well-defined goal or vision. He emphasizes the need to envision our desired outcomes with clarity and specificity. By painting a vivid mental picture of our goals, we activate the creative power of our minds and set the stage for tangible manifestations.

I sat at my desk one day trying to practice this principle. I closed my eyes and tried to visualize my ideal future. *What does success look like for me?* The images that came to mind were both exciting and daunting.

However, mere conception isn't enough. Nightingale's second part, "and believe," highlights the critical role of belief in the achievement process. Belief fuels our actions and propels us forward, even in the face of obstacles. When we genuinely believe in the possibility of our goals, we align our thoughts, emotions, and actions to support their realization.

"Belief is the thermostat that regulates what we accomplish in life," says Nightingale. I realized my own thermostat was set too low.

It's time to turn up the heat!

Nightingale's teaching isn't about wishful thinking or blind optimism; it's about cultivating a deep-rooted faith in our abilities and the potential of our goals. It's about adopting a mindset of unshakable confidence and determination, regardless of external circumstances.

I've faced some obstacles on my journey that seemed insurmountable. And I heard Nightingale's voice in my head: *All you need is the plan, the road map, and the courage to press on to your destination.* It gave me the strength to push through.

The profound truth in this teaching is that our minds are incredibly powerful tools. They have the capacity to shape our reality, influence our decisions, and drive us toward our desired outcomes. By harnessing the power of our minds and aligning our thoughts with our aspirations, we unlock limitless possibilities.

"You become what you think about," Nightingale insisted. This idea was both empowering and terrifying.

If this is true, then I need to be much more careful about what I allow to occupy my mind.

In essence, Nightingale's teaching serves as a timeless reminder of the transformative power of belief and the profound impact it has on our ability to achieve greatness. It encourages us to nurture a positive mindset, cultivate a strong belief in our dreams, and take inspired actions toward their realization.

I'm so grateful for this teaching. It's the lens through which I view challenges, the fuel that drives my ambitions, and the foundation upon which I've built my life and success.

Bless you, Earl, for showing me the power of my own mind. It's a lesson I continue to apply every day, in every aspect of my life.

TRENT TAKEAWAYS

- Create a clear mental picture of your goals and path to success.

- Belief fuels action.

- LEAP–Learn, Exert, Adapt, Persevere (4-step formula).

"The man who moves a mountain begins by carrying away small stones...
It does not matter how slowly you go so long as you do not stop. "

~Confucius

CHAPTER 14

MEASURE

ENTREPRENEURIAL INSPIRATION
The Power of Persistence: How Consistent Effort and Unexpected Connections Can Drive Business Growth

At the end of 2009, the financial crisis was finally well behind us, and the markets and economy gradually stabilized. It was a relief to see things trend in the right direction. As I looked at the improving market charts, I let out a sigh of relief. *We've weathered the storm, but where do we go from here?*

At that point, I was 13 years into my entrepreneurial journey with TCM. However, I felt the need for a tangible way to gauge my progress and maintain regular interaction with my existing partnerships, influential contacts, and potential new clients.

In the world of business, the quote "If you can't measure it, you can't manage it" rings true. This principle became evident as I sought ways to measure my activities and ensure effective management. I remember sitting at my desk, surrounded by reports and charts, feeling overwhelmed.

There has to be a simpler way to track progress.

Drawing from personal development literature and my experiences, I devised a simple yet powerful metric—a minimum of ten meetings with clients, prospects, and centers of influence per week with no exceptions. As I wrote this goal down, I felt a mix of excitement and apprehension.

Can I really commit to this every single week?

This metric provided clarity and structure, helping me track progress and nurture relationships. Each week, I looked at my calendar and asked myself, *Am I on track to meet my goal?*

There was a Thursday evening that stood out. I completed nine appointments by then but was determined to make it a perfect ten. Even though I was in New Hampshire to support my son Carter's basketball game, I couldn't resist reaching out to his coach. He was in his late 20s and not someone I typically considered as a potential client.

As I sat in the hotel room watching Carter mentally prepare for his game, I felt a twinge of guilt. *Should I really be thinking about work right now?* But then I reminded myself of my commitment. *One more meeting, that's all it takes to hit the goal.*

I expressed interest in meeting him to discuss my company, Trent Capital Management. I sent him a quick text: "Hey Pete, I know this is last minute, but I'd love to chat about Trent Capital Management if you have some time tomorrow morning. Let me know if you're available."

As I hit send, I thought, *this will probably just be a formality, checking off a box.* But a part of me hoped for more. *You never know where opportunities might arise.*

To my surprise, Pete responded almost immediately: "Sure, David. I'd be happy to meet. How about 9 AM in my office?"

It turned out to be an incredibly fruitful encounter. Pete not only listened attentively to what I had to say but also went above and beyond by referring me to some of his older friends and family.

As Pete started mentioning names, I got excited. *This is why we push ourselves. You never know where a simple meeting might lead.*

Some of those friends and family became clients. This experience taught me a valuable lesson about the power of setting goals and staying committed. It's a lesson I now eagerly share with my mentees in the world of business and sales.

I often tell them, "Remember the story of my son's basketball coach? That's why we never underestimate any opportunity. Every interaction has potential."

Success often lies just beyond our comfort zone. It's about pushing ourselves to make that one extra call, schedule that one more meeting, even when we think we've done enough.

What if I hadn't reached out to Pete that night? It's a powerful reminder that our most significant opportunities often come from unexpected places, and it's our persistence that uncovers them.

This principle of consistent effort and openness to unexpected connections has become a cornerstone of my business philosophy. It's not just about meeting a quota; it's about cultivating a mindset of constant engagement and opportunity seeking.

As I continue to apply this principle in my business, I'm always excited to see where the next unexpected connection might lead. It's a reminder that in entrepreneurship, every day brings new possibilities if we're willing to reach out and grab them.

FAMILY VALUES
Playful Metrics: How Childhood Contests Can Shape Lifelong Habits and Success

Picture a cozy house nestled in Rose City, where I grew up with my two brothers and sister. Our home boasted three bedrooms and one and a half baths—a small but comfortable setting for our childhood adventures.

As an energetic youngster, I was often outdoors, exploring the nearby recreational complex with its baseball fields and recreation center. I can still feel the excitement of those days, the sun on my face as I raced across the fields. "Just one more game!" I'd plead with my friends as the afternoon light began to fade.

I was a sprightly seven-year-old with my older brother Keith (10). Like many kids, we forgot certain daily routines, including brushing our teeth regularly.

One evening, as we got ready for bed, Mom called out, "David, Keith, did you brush your teeth?"

Keith and I exchanged guilty glances. "Uh, we were just about to," I mumbled, reaching for my toothbrush.

Mom sighed, shaking her head. "We need to find a way to make this a habit," she said, more to herself than us.

Sensing an opportunity for a creative solution, my ingenious mother devised a brilliant plan—a teeth-brushing contest between me and my brother.

The next morning, Mom gathered us in the bathroom. "Boys," she announced, her eyes twinkling with excitement, "we're going to have a contest!"

Keith and I perked up immediately. "What kind of contest?" we asked in unison.

The concept was simple yet effective. She crafted a basic spreadsheet with designated boxes for morning and bedtime brushing, which we diligently marked off each day.

As she taped the paper to the bathroom wall, I felt my competitive spirit. "I'm going to win this," eyeing Keith with a playful grin.

I can't remember the specifics of the prize; what remained vivid is the thrill of healthy competition it ignited.

Every morning and night became a race to the bathroom. "Beat you!" I'd shout, scrambling for my toothbrush.

"Not for long!" Keith replied, hot on my heels.

That water-stained paper taped to the wall, adorned with our daily brush marks and scores, soon became a cherished relic of our childhood. More than just a fun game, the teeth-brushing contest taught us valuable lessons in consistency and commitment. It was a playful way to instill the importance of daily habits. A bit of friendly rivalry motivated us to stay disciplined.

As the days went by, I automatically reached for my toothbrush without being reminded. *It's working*, I realized with surprise. *I actually want to brush my teeth now!*

This simple contest held profound wisdom. It taught me the significance of measuring progress, setting goals, and embracing healthy competition—lessons that stayed with me throughout my life.

Years later, as I sat in my office looking at spreadsheets and performance metrics, I smiled at the memory of that teeth-brushing chart. *Who knew? Mom was preparing us for business all along.*

The experience taught me that even the most mundane tasks can be transformed into engaging challenges with a little creativity. It showed me the power of tracking progress and the motivation that comes from seeing tangible results.

As I apply these lessons in my professional life, setting goals and measuring progress, I often think back to that water-stained chart. It's a reminder that success often starts with small, consistent actions, and that a little friendly competition can be a powerful motivator.

"Thanks, Mom," I whisper sometimes, when I'm setting new targets or reviewing performance metrics. "Your little contest taught me more than you probably ever imagined."

This childhood memory serves as a constant reminder that the foundations of success—discipline, consistency, and the drive to improve—can be instilled in the most playful and unexpected ways. It's a lesson for both my personal life and in my approach to business and mentorship.

MASTER TEACHINGS
Metrics that Matter: Turning Daily Actions into Long-Term Success

Jim Rohn's emphasis on making "measurable progress in reasonable time" resonates deeply. Success isn't just about effort but also about quantifiable results.

I remember watching one of Jim Rohn's seminars, and his words struck a chord. "Success is a numbers game intertwined with consistent action," he said, his voice calm yet powerful. I sat there, nodding along. *He's right. How can I measure my progress more effectively?*

Evaluating personal metrics regularly empowers intentional progress toward long-term goals. Are our daily and weekly actions aligning with our aspirations? These reflections guide us toward intentional steps, knowing each measured move propels us closer to our desired destination.

I found measuring specific, actionable metrics yields the most impactful results. For instance, I track my weekly client interactions, aiming for a minimum of fifteen meaningful engagements now. This could include face-to-face meetings, substantive phone calls, or personalized email exchanges.

One Sunday afternoon, I sat down with my planner, feeling a bit overwhelmed by the week ahead. *How can I ensure I'm making real progress?* Then I remembered Rohn's advice. *Measure your actions, Let's start with client interactions.*

I maintain a simple spreadsheet where I log each interaction, noting the client's name, the nature of our discussion, and any follow-up actions required. As I filled in the details for each meeting, I felt a sense of clarity and control.

This is working, I can see exactly where I need to focus.

Additionally, I measure my personal development efforts. I set a goal to read or listen to at least one business or self-improvement book per week. In my planner, I record the title of the book, key takeaways, and how I plan to implement these insights into my business practices.

I recall a conversation with a colleague who noticed my growing stack of books. "How do you find the time to read so much?" she asked.

"It's all about setting goals and measuring progress," I replied, "I make it a point to read at least one book a week and jot down key takeaways. It keeps me accountable and ensures I'm always learning."

Another crucial metric I monitor is my networking efforts. I aim to attend at least one or two industry events or conferences per quarter. After each event, I track the number of new connections made and follow up with at least three potential collaborators or clients within a week.

After attending a particularly engaging conference, I sat down to review my notes and connections.

Who should I follow up with first?

I decided to start with the three most promising contacts.

This systematic approach is really paying off.

By consistently measuring these key areas—client interactions, personal development, and networking—I can clearly see my progress and identify areas for improvement. This data-driven approach allows me to make informed decisions about where to focus my energy and resources, ensuring my daily actions are aligned with my long-term goals for business growth and personal success.

Reflecting on Rohn's teachings, I often think, *Success isn't just about working hard; it's about working smart and measuring your progress.* His wisdom reminds me that every small, measured step brings me closer to my goals.

As I continue to apply these principles, I feel a sense of empowerment and direction. I'm grateful for the clarity Rohn's teachings have brought to my journey. Rohn's advice has transformed the way I approach my goals and measure success.

This approach hasn't only enhanced my professional growth but also enriched my personal development. It shows the power of metrics and the profound impact they can have on our ability to achieve long-term success.

TRENT TAKEAWAYS

- We first make our habits, then our habits make us.

- Progress creates belief.

- Did you do the work today?

*"Get rid of negative people who bring you down. Surround yourself
with people who lift you up and lend you knowledge and help you learn.
Raise your standards for your inner circle."*

~Tony Robbins

CHAPTER 15

NEED

ENTREPRENEURIAL INSPIRATION

The Art of Discernment:
Mastering Client Selection for Sustainable Success

Around 2006, I encountered a diverse array of clients during the formative stages of my business journey. This spectrum ranged from remarkably rewarding collaborations to more challenging engagements. I secured new business deals that propelled our growth, but I also faced disagreements with vendors and clients that tested my patience and resolve. Like many entrepreneurs, I grappled with the balance between seizing opportunities and managing demanding clients.

One afternoon, I was drained after a meeting. I slumped in my chair, rubbing my temples. *Is this really what I signed up for? There has to be a better way to manage these relationships.*

It wasn't until I reached a decade at Trent Capital Management that I realized the critical importance of discernment in client selection. This realization is summarized in the adage, "You need me a lot more than I need you." Despite the allure of lucrative prospects, I honed my focus on finding clients who aligned with our values and vision, prioritizing synergy over immediate gains.

Among the myriad client experiences, one individual, whom we'll call John, exemplified the complexities of client management. John was affable yet demanding, and often required considerable time and energy from both me and my team. His penchant for constant engagement—sometimes sending almost daily emails—was overwhelming.

As I was about to leave the office one evening, my phone buzzed with yet another email from John. *Not again.* I sighed, feeling the weight of exhaustion. *Is this really worth the stress he's causing my team and me?*

Taking inspiration from Strategic Coach and their refined approach to client dynamics, I remembered the concept of "always be the buyer." This philosophy, articulated by Dan Sullivan, resonated deeply. It's a shift from being a skilled salesperson to embodying the discerning mindset of a buyer in client interactions.

I recall a teaching where Dan spoke about this. "As the buyer, you have the power to choose who you work with," he said. "Don't be afraid to set boundaries and prioritize your well-being."

Maybe it's time to take control of my client relationships, feeling a newfound sense of empowerment.

The pivotal moment came when I initiated an honest conversation with John. I took a deep breath, steeling myself for the discussion. "John, your communication style is creating stress on my team. I think you need to find another firm to assist you," I said, bracing myself for his reaction.

To my surprise, after some conversation, John responded with genuine understanding and empathy. "Thanks, David. I agree we need a more balanced approach," he said, his tone sincere.

I felt a wave of relief. *Why didn't I do this sooner?*

Open communication and mutual respect in client engagements is powerful. This transformative dialogue not only improved our working relationship but also emphasized setting clear boundaries and expectations. This fosters a more productive and harmonious collaboration moving forward.

I learned that quality always trumps quantity when it comes to client relationships. It's not about the sheer number of clients but rather about cultivating meaningful partnerships built on trust, mutual benefit, and shared values.

I often share this lesson with my mentees. "It's better to have a few great clients than a lot of stressful ones," I tell them. "Focus on building relationships that align with your values and vision."

This shift in mindset not only enhanced client interactions but also contributed to the overall success and sustainability of our business endeavors. I'm very grateful to have learned this lesson.

By embracing the art of discernment, I've created a more balanced and fulfilling professional life. It's a lesson that continues to guide me, reminding me that true success lies in the quality of our relationships and the alignment of our values.

Hats off to Dan Sullivan. I appreciate the wisdom that helped me transform my approach to client selection; it's made a world of difference.

FAMILY VALUES

From Caddie to CEO: How Childhood Golf Lessons Shape Business Principles

Dad's childhood memories are filled with adventures at Batesville Country Club. He and his friends, the Ballard and Caldwell boys, spent their days caddying and playing golf. On Wednesdays, Saturdays, and Sundays, they were regulars on the course, sporting patched-up clothes and using cardboard to mend their worn-out shoes.

As Dad recounted these stories, I imagined him as a young boy, full of determination and grit. "How did you manage with such limited resources?" I asked, marveling at his resilience.

Dad's eyes twinkled as he replied, "We made do with what we had. It wasn't about what we didn't have, but what we could do with what we did have."

Dad loved caddying for Ken Williams' wife, who had a light bag and tipped generously. However, his most profitable bag belonged to Glen Edgar, a big-time gambler who paid Dad two dollars plus a cut of his winnings. One day, Dad made around ten dollars when Glen had a successful day.

"Ten dollars!" I exclaimed. "That must have felt like a fortune back then."

Dad nodded, grinning. "Oh, you bet it did. I felt like the richest kid in Batesville that day."

Another memorable experience was traveling with Bob Jennings, the owner of a local grocery store, to caddie at a tournament in Searcy.

Dad cherishes the wonderful memories from his days on the golf course. "I used a hollowed-out tree limb as my first club," he told me. I saw the pride in his eyes as he spoke, and thought: *This is where his entrepreneurial spirit began.*

Eventually, he purchased a 7-iron from Francis Holland for five dollars. Living just half a block away from Dad, Francis was highly respected by everyone in the neighborhood. "It took me some time to gather the money to pay Francis for the club, but I eventually managed it."

I admired Dad's determination. "That must have been a big investment for you," I said.

"It was. But I knew it would pay off in the long run."

Apart from earning money through caddying, Dad also sold golf balls he found for ten cents each.

"Me and my friends each had just one golf club, but together we managed to create a complete set by sharing," Dad continued. "From sunrise to sunset, we hit the course, playing rounds and betting five cent scats." Dad chuckles as he mentions, "Bear Runyon still owes me 15 cents."

I laughed along with him. *Even then, he was learning about partnerships and negotiations.*

Dad's most notorious round involved a day spent with the mayor of Batesville, Harny Chaney. The scorching weather made it even more challenging, and to add to the burden, Harny carried an enormous, weighty leather bag. Despite being a skilled player, Harny had a reputation for being stingy.

After the exhausting round, Dad found solace in munching on crackers and sipping a refreshing Grapette cola. "I couldn't believe after all that, he handed me a measly 50 cents. I was furious." He couldn't help but express his discontent, remarking that it was "pretty damn cheap for the mayor."

As Dad recounted this story, I felt proud. *Even then, you knew your worth.*

Consequently, the golf pro suspended Dad for two weeks, but he never returned. Thus, his short-lived career as a caddie came to an end at the tender age of 14.

Looking back on Dad's experiences, I can't help but see a parallel to the business principle I've come to embrace: "You need me more than I need you." At just 14, Dad instinctively understood his worth and wasn't afraid to stand up for it, even to the mayor.

"Dad," I said, feeling a deep sense of gratitude, "do you realize how much your experiences have shaped our family's values?"

He looked at me, a bit surprised. "How so?"

"Your story with the mayor," I explained. "It's exactly the principle I use in business today. Knowing your worth and being willing to walk away from unfair treatment."

Dad smiled, a mix of pride and nostalgia in his eyes. "Well, I'll be. I guess those golf course lessons were worth more than I thought."

This early lesson in valuing oneself and one's work has echoed through generations, shaping my own approach to client relationships and business dealings. It's a reminder that in both life and business, recognizing your value and being willing to walk away from unfair treatment is crucial for long-term success and self-respect.

As I reflect on Dad's stories, I'm filled with a deep appreciation for the values he unknowingly instilled in me. Thank you, Dad, your childhood experiences on the golf course have become a foundation of our family's business principles.

Success isn't just about skills or opportunities, but about understanding your worth and standing firm in your values. This lesson holds true every day, in every business decision I make.

MASTER TEACHINGS
Beyond Nickel and Dime:
Embracing Self-Worth to Elevate Business Success

In my good friend Justin Breen's book *Epic Business*, he explores a fundamental truth: How we perceive ourselves reflects in our interactions and ultimately shapes our success. The concept of being "nickel and dime" versus valuing oneself is a pivotal distinction that can make or break a business journey.

I remember the day I first read Justin's book. As I turned the pages, his words struck a chord deep within me. *This is it—this is what I've been struggling to articulate all these years.*

When we view ourselves as "nickel and dime," we unconsciously set limits on our potential and worth. This mindset affects our self-esteem and also influences how others perceive and engage with us professionally. It's a cycle that can keep us trapped in a loop of undervaluation and missed opportunities.

I recall times when I undervalued my services. *Was I stuck in a 'nickel and dime' mindset without even realizing it?* It's easy to feel regret.

The term "nickel and dime" carries a weighty connotation in the business world. It refers to a mentality of focusing on small gains or savings at the expense of larger, more significant opportunities. These individuals may seek discounts, haggle over minor details, and generally undervalue the services or products they receive.

I remembered a client who constantly tried to negotiate every aspect of our agreement. "Can't you do it for less?" they'd ask. "Other advisors are offering discounts." At the time, I felt pressured to comply, but now I realize the impact it had on my business and self-worth.

What's striking is how these "nickel and dime" behaviors extend beyond financial transactions. They permeate social circles, networking groups, and online communities, creating an environment where like-minded individuals attract and reinforce each other's beliefs.

At a recent networking event, I overheard a conversation that made me cringe. "I got them to knock off an extra five percent," one person boasted. "Why pay full price when you can negotiate down?" another chimed in. I questioned: *Is this really the path to success?*

From personal experience and corroborated by other sources, it's evident that associating with "nickel and dime" individuals can be toxic for business growth.

Justin's words echoed in my mind: "Your network is your net worth. Surround yourself with people who value what you bring to the table."

Firstly, they may not have the financial capacity to fully appreciate or invest in what you offer, leading to constant negotiations and dissatisfaction. I've had clients ask, "Can you offer a discount?" more times than I can count. Each time, I felt a little piece of my confidence chip away.

Secondly, their propensity to question every decision can drain valuable time and energy, hindering progress and innovation. "Are you sure that's the right way to do this?" they'd ask, making me second-guess my expertise.

Lastly, their referrals are often limited to others who share similar mindsets, perpetuating a cycle of undervaluation and missed opportunities.

As I internalized these lessons, I shifted my mindset.

No more undervaluing my worth, it's vital to attract clients who appreciate the value I bring.

In essence, Justin Breen's insights and the broader wisdom on this topic emphasize the importance of valuing oneself and surrounding oneself with individuals who appreciate and reciprocate that value. By steering clear of the "nickel and dime" mentality, entrepreneurs can create a more conducive environment for growth, collaboration, and sustainable success.

Now, when I mentor young entrepreneurs, I make sure to pass on this valuable lesson. "Remember, your worth isn't determined by how much you can discount. It's about the value you bring to the table."

I'm grateful for the wisdom shared by mentors like Justin. Success isn't just about financial gains—it's about valuing yourself, your skills, and your contributions. And when you do that, the right opportunities and people naturally gravitate towards you.

TRENT TAKEAWAYS

- When you are good to others, you are best to yourself.

- Always be aware: "Who am I around?"

- ANAD–Avoid NADs (nickel and dimers).

"Alone we can do so little; together we can do so much."

~Helen Keller

CHAPTER 16

NETWORK

TRENT ENTREPRENEURIAL JOURNEY
Building Authentic Connections: The True Power of Community Engagement

Throughout my entrepreneurial journey, mentorship was more than just a responsibility; it was a burning passion that propelled me forward. As I guided aspiring advisors and navigated the realms of networking and sales, one principle always stood out: the power of genuine community engagement.

I often encouraged my mentees to immerse themselves in community involvement, but not merely for the sake of building connections. It had to be something they truly believed in and ignited their inner fire. For those with children involved in sports, I had a special recommendation: become their coach.

One day, during a mentoring session, I asked a young advisor, "Do you have any kids involved in sports?"

"Yes," he replied, "my son plays soccer."

"Perfect," I said with a smile. "Why not become his coach? It's not just about the sport; it's about the lessons you can teach and the connections you can make."

Whether it was soccer or basketball, the sport itself took a backseat to the valuable lessons we imparted. As a coach, my focus extended beyond winning games; it encompassed nurturing individual skills and fostering character development. It was during these coaching sessions that I unearthed a remarkable opportunity to instill wisdom beyond the confines of the field.

At the conclusion of each practice, I introduced what I fondly called "Wisdom sessions"—brief yet impactful discussions tailored to the specific age group I coached. We gathered around, and the players took turns reading sections aloud. This not only reinforced the lessons learned but also fostered open discussions and engaging Q&A sessions.

After one tough practice, I gathered the kids around. "Alright, team, today we're going to talk about perseverance."

One of the kids, looking curious, asked, "Coach, what's perseverance?"

"It's about never giving up, no matter how tough things get," I explained. "It's about pushing through the tough stuff and coming out stronger on the other side."

The impact of these sessions extended far beyond the sports field. They taught values like preparation, care, and integrity. Parents admired the holistic approach, and many of them became good friends in addition to clients. It was never about networking; it was always about forging genuine connections and making a positive impact.

Interestingly, some of my mentees from different industries eventually became clients as well. As they grew in their abilities, character, and wisdom, they started to have a profound impact on me, too, teaching me valuable tips and lessons. It doesn't get any better than that.

One day, a former mentee Andrew reached out to me. "David, I just wanted to thank you for all the guidance. I've started implementing those wisdom sessions with my team, and it's made a huge difference."

"That's fantastic, Andrew. It's amazing how these small practices can have such a big impact."

In mentoring sessions, I emphasized this ethos: "Don't network for transactions; engage authentically, pour your heart into what you love, and let the connections grow organically. It's not just about winning clients; it's about building meaningful relationships and leaving a lasting impact."

I often wonder why this approach worked so well. The answer is simple: authenticity. When you genuinely care about others and invest your energy in meaningful ways, the connections are real and lasting.

Networking the right way isn't about collecting business cards; it's about creating a community of support, trust, and mutual growth. It's about making a difference in people's lives and allowing them to make a difference in yours.

TRENT FAMILY TALES
Coaching Avery's Soccer Team:
Building Relationships on and off the Field

When the local YMCA approached me to coach my daughter Avery's 6-year-old soccer team it was an unexpected opportunity to connect and build relationships. This was back in 2000, a bustling time in my business where networking and building meaningful connections were paramount.

Initially, I hesitated. Soccer isn't my forte, and my schedule is already packed with commitments.

However, the YMCA persisted, emphasizing the significance of having a dedicated coach. "Mr. Trent, the kids really need someone who can commit," the coordinator said.

The thought of contributing positively to Avery's team and fostering relationships with the parents and players intrigued me. Could this be a chance to make a difference? So, I decided to dive in and carve out the time.

Our team comprised eight six-year-old girls, a diverse group brought together by chance. Armed with soccer manuals and advice from friends,

I assumed the role of coach. Our practices focused not just on soccer skills but also on teamwork, sportsmanship, and building lasting relationships.

During our first practice, I gathered the girls around. "Alright team, we're going to have fun and learn a lot," I said, trying to sound confident. "But most importantly, we're going to work together and support each other."

We implemented creative techniques like using basketball goggles to encourage the girls to keep their heads up while dribbling. One day, as we practiced passing, I noticed Avery struggling.

"Dad, I can't do it," she said, frustrated.

I knelt down to her level. "Avery, it's okay to find things hard. Just keep your head up and try again. Remember, it's about effort, not perfection."

We practiced passing, shooting, and emphasized playing with determination and humility, instilling values that extended beyond the field.

As our early practices progressed, the team bonded deeply, nicknaming themselves "The Monsters" to amplify their camaraderie. Each player received playful nicknames like Bruiser Berry, Turbo Twins, Little Engine, and Rooster, adding a fun element to the experience.

One day, after a particularly tough game, I gathered the girls. "Monsters, you played with heart today," I said, proud. "Win or lose, it's your effort and teamwork that matter most."

What began as a commitment for one season flourished into four, spanning two years of fall and spring seasons. The Monsters evolved into a formidable team, *undefeated* throughout all four seasons, and radiated joy both during games and off the field.

I'm immensely grateful for the networking opportunities and relationships that blossomed. Interacting with parents, fellow coaches, and witnessing the growth of the young players not only enriched Avery's experience but also mine.

One evening, after a game, a parent approached me. "David, thank you for everything. My daughter has grown so much under your coaching," she said, grateful.

I smiled, feeling fulfilled. "It's been a pleasure. These girls have taught me as much as I've taught them."

Even today, encountering those young ladies, now in their early 30s, brings back cherished memories and reaffirms the power of networking and building relationships, both professionally and personally.

I ran into a former player at a local event and she exclaimed, "Coach Trent! Remember when we were The Monsters?"

I laughed, feeling a rush of nostalgia. "How could I forget? You all were the best team I ever coached."

These experiences taught me that true networking isn't just about business; it's about forming genuine connections and making a positive impact on the lives of others. Coaching Avery's soccer team was one of the most rewarding endeavors of my life, and the relationships formed during those years continue to enrich my journey.

MASTER TEACHINGS
Mike Garrison's "Can I Borrow Your Car?": The Art of Authentic Networking

After years of practicing networking principles intuitively, I recently came across Mike Garrison's book *Can I Borrow Your Car?* It was a revelation—a structured approach to many of the networking strategies I used throughout my career. This book validated my methods and provided fresh insights I wish I knew earlier.

Mike's approach to networking aligns perfectly with the principles I've discussed in my experiences with coaching Avery's soccer team and mentoring young professionals. Here are some key takeaways from *Can I Borrow Your Car?* that resonate strongly:

Authentic Engagement: Mike emphasizes the importance of genuine connections, much like how I approached coaching and mentoring. It's not about collecting business cards; it's about building real relationships.

Giving Before Receiving: This principle mirrors my approach to community involvement. By volunteering as a coach and mentor, I was giving value to others without expectation of immediate return.

The Power of Stories: Mike highlights how sharing personal stories can create deeper connections. This reminds me of the "Wisdom sessions" I held with the soccer team, where we shared experiences and lessons learned.

Long-Term Relationship Building: The book stresses the importance of nurturing relationships over time, similar to how my connections with the soccer parents and players lasted well beyond our seasons together.

Creating Memorable Experiences: Mike talks about creating unique experiences to stand out. This is what we did when we created special moments for "The Monsters" soccer team, like giving them nicknames and using creative training techniques.

Follow-Up and Consistency: The book emphasizes the importance of consistent follow-up, which aligns with how I maintained relationships with mentees and clients over the years.

Reading *Can I Borrow Your Car?* was like finding a roadmap for the journey I was already on. It provided structure and terminology for practices I developed through experience. For instance, Mike's concept of "relationship currency" perfectly describes the goodwill I built through coaching and mentoring.

One particular passage from the book struck me: "Networking isn't about making sales; it's about making friends." This encapsulates my approach throughout my career, from coaching soccer to mentoring young professionals.

I found myself nodding in agreement as I read about Mike's strategies for creating meaningful connections. It reminded me of a conversation I had with a parent after a soccer game:

"You know, David," she said, "I came here expecting just soccer lessons for my daughter, but you've given us so much more—a community, life lessons, and lasting friendships."

I realized many of Mike's teachings were principles I intuitively followed. I was so intrigued by Mike Garrison's insights that I reached out to him directly. To my delight, Mike was incredibly approachable and generous with his time.

"Mike, your book has really changed my perspective on networking," I told him during our first conversation. "I feel like I've been practicing these principles without even knowing it."

"I'm glad to hear that, David," he replied warmly. "Networking is about building real relationships, and it sounds like you're already on that path."

In the end, my relationship with Mike Garrison exemplifies the very essence of what I've learned about networking: when you engage authentically and invest in meaningful connections, the rewards extend far beyond what you initially anticipate.

In essence, *Can I Borrow Your Car?* serves as a powerful guide for anyone looking to master the art of authentic networking. It's a reminder that true networking is about building relationships, adding value, and creating lasting connections—principles at the core of my journey in business and life.

TRENT TAKEAWAYS

- Strive for quality connections over quantity.

- Coming together is a beginning; keeping together is progress; working together is success.

- Help Others with No Expectation.

"The greatest use of a life is to spend it on something that will outlast it."

~William James

CHAPTER 17

INVEST (IN OTHERS)

ENTREPRENEURIAL INSPIRATION
The Ripple Effect of Mentorship: How Guiding Others Can Transform Lives and Businesses

In 2017, I crossed paths with Chris Chunn, who was 24 years my junior, and my entrepreneurial journey took a significant turn. After several attempts at cold calling, Chris finally reached me, and it was a memorable conversation.

"Hi Mr. Trent. I'm Chris Chunn. It's great to meet you. I have a potential candidate I'd like you to meet," his voice came through the phone, confident yet respectful.

Another cold call. But there's something different about this one. Intrigued by his approach, I agreed to meet him.

Our initial meeting exceeded expectations. Beyond his professional capabilities, we discovered common ground, including attending the same high school.

"You went to North Little Rock High too?" I asked, feeling a sudden connection.

Chris nodded, his eyes lighting up. "Class of 2009. It's a small world, isn't it?"

Chris, then a recruiter at a Fortune 500 Recruiting Company, impressed me, not only with his calm demeanor, but also with his determination to excel and support me in any way he could. His "eat what you kill" ethos aligned with my entrepreneurial spirit.

This young man has something special. He reminds me of myself at his age.

Our friendship blossomed into mentorship, with Chris absorbing the book recommendations I shared and reciprocating with impactful reads of his own. Over the years, I've witnessed his personal milestones, from marriage to the birth of his children, all while nurturing our professional rapport.

I remember the day Chris told me about his engagement. "David, I'm getting married!" he exclaimed, his voice joyful.

"That's wonderful, Chris," I replied. I felt proud, as if he were my own son. "Life is about to get even more exciting."

Encouraging Chris to pursue entrepreneurship became a recurring theme in our conversations. After careful consideration, he and his partner, Stephanie Shine, launched Arkansas Talent Group in March 2024.

"Are you sure you're ready for this?" I asked Chris one day, wanting to ensure he understood what lay ahead.

"I am," he replied, his voice steady with determination. "And I have you to thank for giving me the confidence to take this leap."

Chris's growth has been remarkable, and our relationship has evolved into mutual mentorship. His recent text, quoting Alex Hormozi and crediting me for his decision to start his own company, reflects the value of supportive relationships in achieving goals: "Here is a quote from Alex Hormozi: 'The rare people in your life who root for you to hit your goals are more valuable than the goals themselves.' My mom asked me this weekend what drove me to finally pull the trigger and start my own company. I told her David Trent played a big part of it!"

As I read his message, I felt a lump in my throat. *Is this really the impact I've had?* I felt humbled, proud, and overwhelmed.

This message meant the world to me. It reaffirmed the impact of mentorship and support in empowering others to pursue their dreams.

Chris has taught me as much as I've taught him. His success is a result of his abilities and also to the power of meaningful connections and shared aspirations.

This is why we do what we do, it's not just about our own success, but about lifting others up along the way.

The purpose-filled experience with Chris has reinforced my belief in the power of mentorship. It showed me that by investing in others, we help them grow and also continue our own growth journey. It's a beautiful cycle of learning, sharing, and mutual success.

I'm grateful for the lessons Chris taught me about the impact of genuine connection and support. He has reminded me of the true meaning of success.

This journey with Chris is a powerful reminder that our greatest achievements often come not from what we accomplish alone, but from the lives we touch and the potential we help unlock in others.

FAMILY VALUES

Teaching with Heart: How One Sunday School Teacher Transformed Lives Through Compassion and Empathy

My mother, Donnie Lou, was a shining example of "Elevating Others", as a dedicated Sunday school teacher. I have a vivid memory of Saturday nights spent watching her prepare lessons for her classes the next day (yes, she was a bit of a procrastinator).

I remember one Saturday evening, peeking into her study. "Mom, it's getting late. Shouldn't you be resting for tomorrow?" I asked, concerned.

She looked up from her notes, a warm smile on her face. "Oh, David, there's always time to make a difference in these kids' lives. I'll rest when I'm done."

I admired her dedication. *How does she do it week after week?* I felt awe and concern.

She taught teenagers and continued to do so even as she got older, but for this story, I'll focus on the teenagers.

On Sunday mornings, Mom eagerly awaited the arrival of her students. Being a Sunday school teacher was more than just a duty for her; it was a calling—a chance to positively impact the lives of teenagers. In later life, she taught her peers. She believed in the power of education, not just academically but spiritually and morally as well. Through engaging lessons, interactive activities, and heartfelt conversations, Mom aimed to instill values of kindness, compassion, and empathy in her students.

What kept Mom going was the transformation she witnessed in her students. They blossomed into thoughtful individuals, showing newfound understanding and respect for others, embodying the values she so passionately imparted. The camaraderie among her students expanded into a tight-knit community, a safe harbor where personal growth and spiritual exploration flourished.

Mom often shared stories with me about her experiences and her eyes lit up when she talked. "David, seeing those kids grow and change was the best reward. I remember one student, Suzan, who came in so shy and withdrawn. By the end of the year, she was leading discussions and helping others. It was incredible to watch."

I felt so proud as I listened to her stories. *She's not just teaching, she's changing lives.*

"Mom," I asked one day, "what do you think made the biggest difference for Suzan?"

She smiled warmly, thinking back. "I think it was just letting her know that she was valued and that her voice mattered. Once she felt that, she started to come out of her shell."

Isn't that what we all need? To feel valued and heard?

Mom not only impacted her students but also experienced personal growth and fulfillment. Teaching required patience, empathy, and creativity—qualities she continued to develop with each lesson. I remember some of my peers and friends who Mom taught expressing gratitude for her guidance and sharing how she had inspired them. Mom truly understood the profound impact of her role as a Sunday school teacher.

"I always told them," Mom would say, her voice filled with conviction, "It's not just about learning the lessons; it's about living them. If you can take what we talk about here and apply it out there in the world, then I've done my job."

"That's a powerful message, Mom," I replied, feeling the weight of her words. "It's something we can all strive to do."

As I listened to her, I knew: *She's not just teaching Sunday school, she's teaching life lessons. How many of us truly live what we learn?*

Mom found joy in dedicating herself to teaching; understanding each lesson, conversation, and smile held the potential to change lives and foster a kinder, more empathetic world.

Watching her over the years, I realized the profound impact one person can have when they dedicate themselves to the good of others.

Mom's legacy isn't just in the lessons she taught but in the lives she touched and the kindness she inspired.

Her dedication to teaching has been a guide for me, reminding me that true success isn't measured by personal achievements but by the positive impact we have on others. It's another lasting lesson in my business dealings and personal relationships, always striving to embody the values she so tirelessly taught.

"Thank you, Mom," I whisper sometimes, feeling grateful for the example she set. "You've shown me what it truly means to make a difference in this world."

MASTER TEACHINGS
The Ripple Effect of Caring:
How Helping Others Leads to
Personal and Professional Fulfillment

Zig Ziglar's wisdom shines brightly in the world of personal growth and leadership, highlighting the power of caring for and supporting others. "You can have everything in life you want if you will just help other people get what they want," is the essence of this philosophy.

I remember the first time I heard this quote at a seminar. Ziglar's voice was filled with conviction as he said it. It was like a light bulb went off in my head. *Is it really that simple? Can helping others truly lead to my own success?*

THE RIPPLE EFFECT

When we adopt Ziglar's teachings and prioritize being interested in and investing in others, it sets off a powerful ripple effect which brings forth positive outcomes, fostering a culture of collaboration, support, and empowerment. It creates an environment where everyone can thrive and achieve their goals.

I remember putting this into practice with a mentee. "Billy, what's your biggest challenge right now?" As he opened up, I felt a shift in our relationship. By focusing on his needs, I strengthened our bond.

"David, I just can't seem to get my team motivated," Billy confessed, looking frustrated.

"Let's work on that together," I replied, feeling a sense of purpose. "We'll find a way to inspire them."

PRACTICAL STRATEGIES FOR SUCCESS

Ziglar's approach offers practical strategies that lead to success.

Active Listening: By practicing attentive listening, we can better understand others' perspectives and needs.

I remember Ziglar saying, "You never know when a moment and a few sincere words can have an impact on a life." I made a conscious effort to listen more intently in my interactions.

Empathy and Understanding: Putting ourselves in others' shoes allows us to empathize with their experiences.

"People don't care how much you know until they know how much you care." Ziglar's words echoed in my mind as I navigated a difficult conversation with a team member.

Support and Encouragement: Offering genuine support, encouragement, and positive feedback inspires others to reach their full potential.

Mentorship and Guidance: Sharing our knowledge, expertise, and guidance helps others succeed.

Recognition and Appreciation: Acknowledging and appreciating others' contributions and achievements boosts morale and motivation.

I started implementing these strategies in my daily life. *How can I support my team better?* I asked myself each morning. The results were transformative.

CREATING A LIFE OF FULFILLMENT

By embodying Ziglar's teachings and actively being interested in and investing in others, we contribute to the success of those around us and also experience personal growth, fulfillment, and satisfaction ourselves. It's a win-win approach that fosters a culture of positivity, collaboration, and continuous improvement.

One day, after helping a colleague through a very tough situation, I felt an overwhelming sense of satisfaction. *This is what Ziglar meant. By helping others, I'm finding my own fulfillment.*

Ziglar's voice seemed to speak to me: "You will get all you want in life if you help enough other people get what they want." I felt a renewed sense of purpose.

Let's embrace the Ziglar approach and make a difference in the lives of others. As I continue to apply these principles in my personal and professional life, I'm constantly amazed at the doors that open, not just for others, but for myself as well.

This philosophy is more than just a business strategy; it's a way of life. Our greatest achievements often come not from what we accomplish, but from the lives we touch and the potential we help unlock in others.

As I mentor young entrepreneurs or lead my team, I always come back to Ziglar's wisdom. "Remember," I tell them, "your success is directly tied to how much you invest in others." It's a powerful reminder that in business and in life, we rise by lifting others.

TRENT TAKEAWAYS

- Teaching can be transformative.

- Acknowledge and celebrate the achievements of those you mentor.

- FAITH – Forge Ahead with Intention, Tenacity, and Hope.

"And Jabez called on the God of Israel saying, 'Oh, that You would bless me indeed, enlarge my territory, that Your hand would be with me, and that You would keep me from evil, that I may not cause pain!', So God granted him what he requested."

~1 Chronicles 4:10

CHAPTER 18

PRAYER

ENTREPRENEURIAL INSPIRATION

Divine Connections:
How Faith and Philanthropy
Can Transform Lives and Communities

In 2018, I had the remarkable opportunity to reconnect with an old acquaintance from my junior high and high school days—Larry Clark. Despite not being particularly close in our younger years, something inexplicable clicked between us as we met again in our mid-50s.

Why didn't we connect like this back then? What's changed?

Little did I know about Larry's incredible journey or the profound impact his Christian faith had on his life. I was immediately struck by his boundless energy, unfaltering faith in God, and passionate dedication to the nonprofit organization he founded in 2007. What drew Larry and me together wasn't just our shared entrepreneurial spirit but also his unique focus on philanthropy.

"David," Larry said during one of our early conversations, his eyes shining with enthusiasm, "It was a divine calling that propelled me to start this journey in 2006. I felt God's hand guiding me every step of the way."

I was intrigued. "What made you take that leap, Larry?" I asked, leaning in.

He smiled. "By 2007, I knew I had to take decisive action. As 'Coach Clark,' I've been mentoring young people for years. I saw firsthand the critical need for year-round educational opportunities and support services for children and families."

This is what true purpose looks like. How can I find that level of passion in my own work?

Starting with a small group of children at a local Boys' Club in 2007, the impact of his efforts was nothing short of extraordinary. Over the years, his organization, Life Skills for Youth (LSY), positively influenced the lives of more than 4,000 young people, provided an incredible 1,562,100 million healthy meals and snacks, and brought significant positive changes to numerous families.

"That's incredible, Larry," I remarked, genuinely impressed. "How do you maintain your drive and enthusiasm?"

Larry leaned forward with conviction. "It's all about faith, David. Let me introduce you to something that's been transformative for me."

What could be so powerful?»

Larry introduced me to a book called *The Prayer of Jabez* by Bruce Wilkinson. This prayer, inspired by 1 Chronicles 4:10, has been a revelation, showing me the path to receiving God's blessings and protection, just as Jabez did.

"David, this prayer has changed my life," Larry explained with sincerity. "It's simple but powerful. Let me share it with you."

He then recited the four-part prayer: "Oh that You would bless me indeed (1) and enlarge my territory (2) Let Your hand be with me (3) and keep me from the evil one (4)."

As I listened, I felt a strange sense of peace. *Could something so simple really be so powerful?*

The impact of this prayer has been profound and immeasurable, transforming my perspective and approach to life. I pray this prayer multiple times daily, finding immense comfort and guidance in its words as I navigate each day.

"Larry," I confided one day, feeling a deep sense of gratitude, "I can't thank you enough for sharing this with me. It's become an integral part of my daily life."

He nodded with a warm smile. "That's the beauty of faith, David. When we share it, it grows and touches more lives than we could ever imagine on our own."

As I reflected on Larry's words, I realized this is about more than just business success. It's about making a real difference in the world.

Larry Clark's entrepreneurial spirit, infused with a deep commitment to philanthropy, created a ripple effect of positive change that continues to touch and transform the lives of countless individuals and families. One person can have an incredible impact when driven by faith, passion, and a genuine desire to make a difference in the world.

I often think back to my conversations with Larry. *How can I incorporate this level of purpose and faith into my own work?* It's a question that continues to shape my life, reminding me that true success is measured not just in profits, but in the lives we touch and the positive change we create in the world.

FAMILY VALUES

The Silent Sermon: How My Father's Nightly Prayer Ritual Shaped My Faith.

Transitioning from the profound impact of "The Prayer of Jabez," my mind often drifts back to my years in Rose City, where I witnessed a nightly ritual that left an indelible mark on my heart and soul. It was a simple, yet powerful act performed by my father in our small living room, a space that was often overlooked but filled with deep meaning.

Almost every evening, as the sun dipped below the horizon and shadows danced across our living room, my father assumed a humble position on our green-patterned couch. With reverence and devotion, he lowered himself to his hands and knees and bowed his head in prayer to the Lord. In those moments, I sensed the weight of his prayers and the earnestness in his voice even though he spoke silently.

"Dad," I asked softly, "why do you pray like that every night?"

He looked at me with gentle eyes and replied, "Son, it's my way of showing respect to God. When I'm on my knees, I remember how big He is and how much I need Him."

I marveled at his determined faith and belief in God as his Father and friend. It was evident that this connection gave him the strength to face life with resilience and hope. As a child, I couldn't comprehend the depth of his prayers, but knew they encompassed the struggles he faced as the pillar of our family, along with expressions of gratitude for the blessings we enjoyed.

"What do you talk to God about?" I asked another time.

Dad smiled warmly. "Everything, David. Our worries, our joys, our hopes. I thank Him for all we have and ask for His guidance in all we do."

As I watched him, I was in awe. *He's not just praying; he's having a conversation with God.*

The image of my father in prayer in his silent conversations with God was a model for my spiritual journey. It taught me the power of humility, the importance of seeking guidance and solace in prayer, and the impact of faith on one's outlook toward life. This memory guides me, especially during challenging times when I turn to prayer for strength and clarity.

I often remind myself of the acronym KAP (Kneel And Pray). It's not just the physical act of kneeling but also a mindset of humility, surrender, and trust in a higher power. My father's nightly ritual constantly reminds me of the enduring power of faith and the transformative nature of prayer.

Years later, I shared this memory with my father. "Dad, do you know how much your nightly prayers impacted me?" I asked, feeling a mix of nostalgia and gratitude.

He looked surprised. "I didn't realize you noticed, son. I was just doing what felt right."

"It taught me more than you know. It showed me what real faith looks like."

He smiled. "I'm glad, David. Faith has always been my anchor, and I'm happy it could be yours too."

This simple yet profound act of faith is a guiding principle in my life, reminding me that no matter what we face, there's always a higher power to lean on. My father's silent sermons left a lasting legacy.

MASTER TEACHINGS
Built for Challenges: The Transformative Power of Faith, Prayer, and Resilience

Ed Mylett, a prominent entrepreneur, peak performance expert, and motivational speaker, became a newer but deeply impactful voice in my life over the past few years. His teachings on faith, resilience, and the power of prayer resonate deeply. Ed's journey to success is marked by his single-minded faith and commitment to personal growth.

Born and raised in Diamond Bar, California, Ed grew up with a strong sense of determination and a relentless drive to succeed. He began his entrepreneurial journey at a young age and quickly rose to prominence in the finance and real estate industries. Today, he's widely recognized as a leading authority on leadership, personal development, and achieving peak performance.

In a recent podcast, Ed shared insights into his prayer life, describing prayer as his anchor and source of strength. "Prayer is my fortress and safe haven. As I've grown older, my faith has only deepened. I find solace in the saying, 'Jesus take the wheel,' which describes my trust and surrender to a higher power."

As I listened to his words, I felt a deep connection. *That's exactly how I feel; prayer has always been my anchor too.*

Each night, Ed kneels in prayer, pouring out his heart and seeking peace, strength, and discernment. Rather than asking for things to be easier, he prays to become better equipped to handle challenges. "I don't pray for an easy life," Ed said. "I pray for the strength to endure a difficult one."

During another time in my business when I felt overwhelmed, Ed's words came through. *Maybe I need to change my approach. Instead of asking for the problems to go away, I should be asking for the strength to face them.*

During moments of major stress, Ed turns to his faith as a Christian for strength and guidance. He focuses on what he can control and strives not to be overwhelmed by what he cannot. His mantra, "I am built for this," reflects his resilience and belief in overcoming obstacles with faith and determination.

One evening when I was feeling stressed, I decided to try Ed's approach. Kneeling down, I prayed, "God, give me the strength to handle these challenges. Help me to see that I am built for this."

Ed's teachings on faith remind us of the power of surrender, resilience, and trust in a higher purpose. His journey shows the transformative impact of faith and prayer in navigating life and achieving personal growth.

Reflecting on his journey, Ed shared, "You're one decision, one relationship, one thought, one new emotion, one interview, one book away from completely changing your life, but you will never see those one mores if you hold onto these things that don't serve you."

As I pondered his words, I felt a sense of clarity. *What am I holding onto that's not serving me? What changes do I need to make to move forward?*

I had the chance to meet Ed at a conference. I approached him after his talk. "Ed, your teachings have had a profound impact on my life," I said with gratitude and admiration.

"Thank you, David. Remember, you are built for this. Keep the faith, and you'll find the strength you need."

I walked away and felt a renewed purpose. "I am built for this," I repeated to myself. "With faith and resilience, I can face any challenge."

TRENT TAKEAWAYS

- GF2–God is my Father and friend.

- Kneel And Pray (KAP).

- Remind yourself through prayer–"I am built for this."

REFLECTION ON THE LEGACY

MY LATE 50s AND LATER YEARS AT TRENT CAPITAL MANAGEMENT–EMBRACING WISDOM AND PERSPECTIVE

"Yet I will not fail, as the others, for in my hands I now hold the charts, which will guide me through perilous waters to shores, which only yesterday seemed but a dream."

~Og Mandino

CHAPTER 19

CHALLENGES

ENTREPRENEURIAL INSPIRATION
Navigating Uncertainty:
Lessons in Resilience from Financial Crises

The realm of behavioral finance is fraught with various risks, with event risk being one of the most daunting issues to tackle in the portfolio management landscape. These events often catch us off guard, making them particularly tricky to navigate. Three such events in 1999-2000, 2007-2008, and 2020 shaped my journey.

THE Y2K BUG (1999-2000)

In 1999, the first major event appeared in the form of the looming Y2K issue. As the world geared up for the new millennium, concerns about the Y2K bug spread like wildfire. Computer systems and financial institutions scrambled to address potential chaos as the clock ticked closer to January 1, 2000.

Amidst the frenzy, I reassured many anxious clients, calming their fears about the impact of the Y2K bug on their investments. I remember telling one worried client, "Remember, this is a technical issue, not a fundamental economic problem. Our investments are based on solid companies that will continue to operate regardless of the date on the calendar."

Despite my reassurances, one client chose to liquidate their portfolio out of panic. I vividly recall our conversation.

"Are you sure you want to do this?" I asked, trying to keep my voice calm. "The market has been performing well, and pulling out now could mean missing out on potential gains."

"I know," they replied, "but I'd rather be safe than sorry. I can't sleep at night worrying about this Y2K thing." I heard their anxiety.

I hung up the phone and thought: *I hope they don't regret this decision. Sometimes fear can cloud our judgment.*

Despite this minor setback and a few glitches, the transition to the new year proved to be smoother than anticipated, thanks to collective efforts to resolve the Y2K problem.

THE GLOBAL ECONOMIC CRISIS (2007-2009)

Another storm that emerged was in the form of the Global Economic Crisis (GEC) of 2007-2008. This crisis, triggered by a combination of predatory lending practices, risky behavior by financial institutions, and the bursting of the United States housing market bubble, sent shockwaves through the global economy. It was a perfect storm that resulted in the most severe economic downturn since the Great Depression, leading to what is now known as the Great Recession.

Navigating the financial landscape became increasingly demanding during this tumultuous period, requiring strategic decision-making and resilience. Again, comforting and communicating with clients during this time was critical, and we traversed it very successfully as the markets finally rebounded in early 2009.

"David, my portfolio is down 35%. What should I do?" they asked with desperation.

"Stay calm," I replied, trying to project confidence. "We've built a diversified portfolio for a reason. Selling now would lock in losses. Let's focus on the long-term strategy."

As I spoke, I surmised, "This is the toughest period I've ever faced. But I have to stay strong for my clients."

THE COVID-19 PANDEMIC (2020)

As if facing the Y2K bug and the Global Economic Crisis weren't enough, the world was later hit by challenge number three: the COVID-19 pandemic. The onset of the pandemic in 2020 triggered the largest economic crisis in over a century, disrupting industries, economies, and livelihoods on a global scale. The pandemic exacerbated existing inequalities within nations and across the globe, posing unprecedented challenges for businesses and individuals alike.

Again, I remember a particularly anxious call from a long-time client during the early days of the pandemic. "David, the market is plummeting, and I'm really worried about my investments. Should we pull out now before it gets worse?"

"Take a deep breath," I replied. I repeated the same message, "I understand your concerns, but remember, we've built a diversified portfolio designed to weather storms like this. Panic selling now could lock in losses that we might recover from later."

"But what if things don't get better?" they asked. Their voice trembled.

"Historically, markets have *always* rebounded after crises," I reassured them. "Our focus should be on long-term goals. Let's stay the course and trust the strategy we've put in place."

I hung up and reflected. *This is another test of resilience. I have to believe in the strategies we've built and convey that confidence to my clients.*

LESSONS LEARNED

Despite the enormity, each challenge prepared me for the obstacles that lay ahead. Through resilience, adaptability, and a steadfast commitment to guiding clients through turbulent times, I successfully navigated these crises, emerging stronger and more prepared for whatever the future may hold.

Looking back, I can see how I was equipped for what followed. The Y2K scare taught me the importance of clear communication and staying calm in the face of widespread panic. The 2008 financial crisis honed my skills in strategic portfolio management during severe economic downturns. And the COVID-19 pandemic reinforced the value of adaptability and the need for diversification in an increasingly interconnected global economy.

Each past crisis strengthened my ability to analyze complex situations, communicate effectively with clients, and make sound decisions in uncertain times. These experiences have shaped my professional journey and deepened my understanding of resilience and the importance of staying true to a well-thought-out strategy, even when the world seems to be falling apart.

FAMILY VALUES

From Pecans to Perseverance:
How a Family's Strength Overcame Adversity

My grandfather, known to us as PaPaw, embodied the essence of hard work and resilience despite having only completed the third grade. His life was a model of the power of dedication and diligence. His journey began at a mill, where he worked alongside his brother Lonnie and brother-in-law, Long Boy Shelton. This mill job was the beginning of PaPaw's legacy of hard work and resourcefulness.

I admired PaPaw, and as I listened to his stories, I was often curious: *How did he manage to achieve so much with so little formal education?*

My father recounted PaPaw's unique talent for gathering and selling pecans, turning them into a valuable source of income. "I can still see my dad (PaPaw) in my mind's eye," Dad would say with admiration. "He'd climb those trees with his frailing pole, moving like a squirrel despite his small size. The pecans would rain down, and there I'd be, standing below with my toy army helmet on, trying not to get bonked on the head!"

I was in awe (and slightly amused) picturing the scene. *PaPaw must have been quite a sight. I wish I could have seen him in action.*

Dad's eyes twinkled as he continued, "PaPaw was something else. He may have been small, but he was strong and quick. Watching him work those trees was like watching a master at his craft. And those pecans? They were more than just nuts to us—they were a way to make ends meet when times were tough."

As I listened, I felt a deep growing respect. *PaPaw turned a simple task into a lifeline for his family. That's true resourcefulness.*

In 1944, the mill abruptly and unexpectedly closed its doors, plunging the family into financial uncertainty. PaPaw faced this challenge head-on, making the difficult decision to relocate the family to Camden, Arkansas, where he found employment in the defense industry. The transition was tough, but PaPaw's resilience and determination kept the family afloat.

I imagined the stress PaPaw must have felt. *How did he find the strength to uproot his entire family? That must have taken incredible courage.*

After six months of hard work and perseverance, the Trent family rebounded and resettled in Batesville. PaPaw secured a job with the city, working at the cemetery, albeit for a modest wage of 60 cents per hour. "PaPaw used a jackhammer to dig graves," Dad said. This task showcases the physical demands of the job and PaPaw's dedication.

"Dad," I asked, feeling curious, "wasn't that incredibly hard work for PaPaw?"

Dad nodded solemnly. "It was, son. I remember watching PaPaw's body vibrating from the powerful machine. It was tough to see, but PaPaw never complained. He just kept going, day after day."

This vision left a lasting impression on my father, and as he shared it with me, I felt a lump in my throat. *PaPaw's strength wasn't just physical, it was mental and emotional too.*

Resilience and strength defined PaPaw's character and I felt deep respect and gratitude. *PaPaw's struggles and triumphs shaped our family, his perseverance in the face of adversity set a standard for all of us.*

I turned to Dad, feeling a sudden urge to express my thoughts. "Dad, PaPaw's story—it's incredible. How do you think his experiences shaped our family?"

Dad smiled. "David, PaPaw taught us that no matter how tough things get, you keep going. You find a way. That's the Trent way, and it's something I hope you'll always remember."

As I absorbed Dad's words, I felt renewed purpose and determination. PaPaw's legacy wasn't just about hard work; it was about facing life with courage and resourcefulness. It was a lesson I vowed to carry with me, a family value that continued to shape my journey.

"Thank you for sharing these stories, Dad," I said, feeling a deep connection to my family's history. "I'll make sure to pass them on to my own children someday."

PaPaw's journey from pecan gatherer to cemetery worker, and everything in between, became more than just family lore. It became a source of inspiration, a reminder of the strength that runs in our family's veins, and a call to face my own life with the same resilience and determination PaPaw demonstrated.

MASTER TEACHINGS

Living with Purpose:
Embracing Love, Presence, and Emotional Mastery

The Greatest Salesman in the World, penned by Og Mandino in 1968, is more than just a book to me; it's a treasured companion that guided me through the hardest times of my life. Its timeless wisdom (especially the ten scrolls) left an indelible mark.

I remember the day I first picked up the book. *Is this really going to be different from all the other self-help books I've read?* Little did I know how profoundly it would shape my life.

Each scroll, filled with profound insights and life lessons, aligns perfectly with the essence of this chapter. If you ever have the opportunity to listen to Og Mandino reading these scrolls in an audio version, seize it. His captivating voice adds an extra layer of depth and meaning to the profound teachings, making them unforgettable and impactful. Below are three excerpts from the book.

"I will greet this day with love in my heart."

The first time I read this line, I paused. *Love? Even on the tough days?* But as I incorporated this into my daily routine, I realized its power.

This simple yet powerful declaration has been important in my daily routine. Embracing each day with love allows me to approach everything that happens with a positive mindset and a compassionate heart. It reminds me to react to the actions of others with kindness and to let adversity and discouragement become like the softest of rains.

During a difficult meeting with a client, as tensions rose, I took a deep breath and reminded myself: *Greet this with love.* The shift in my approach was palpable, and the situation diffused almost immediately.

This mindset helped me build stronger relationships and maintain a sense of peace even in difficult times.

"I will live this day as if it is my last."

When I first encountered this line, it felt cliché. But then Mandino's voice came through: "To waste this day would be to give up a treasure which can never be regained." It hit me hard.

This line profoundly influenced my life. By focusing on the present and not dwelling on the past or worrying about the future, I can fully engage with each moment. This philosophy encourages me to make the most of every day, appreciating the small joys and tackling tasks with a sense of urgency and purpose.

One morning, as I was rushing through breakfast, barely tasting my food, I stopped.

What if this were my last meal?

From that moment on, I made a conscious effort to savor every bite, every conversation, every moment. It has taught me to let go of unnecessary worries and to cherish the time I have with loved ones.

"Today I will be master of my emotions."

I remember laughing when I first read this. *Master my emotions? Easier said than done.* But as I delved deeper into Mandino's teachings, I understood.

Understanding that emotions ebb and flow like the tides has been crucial in managing my responses to life's ups and downs. Recognizing that moods will rise and fall, I strive to remain balanced and not let temporary feelings dictate my actions.

One stressful day, I found myself on the verge of making a rash decision. Then Mandino's words came to me: "If I feel depressed, I will sing. If I feel sad, I will laugh. If I feel fear, I will plunge ahead." I took a deep breath, stepped back, and approached the situation with a clearer mind.

This teaching helps me maintain a steady course through personal and professional challenges, and allows me to act with clarity and purpose rather than being swayed by fleeting emotions.

Og Mandino's teachings have woven themselves into the fabric of my life, guiding me through both ordinary and extraordinary days. By incorporating these principles, I found a deeper level of fulfillment and resilience.

As I reflect on the impact of *The Greatest Salesman in the World*, I'm filled with gratitude. Bless you, Og; you've given me tools not just for success but for a life well-lived.

The wisdom contained in this book continues to inspire me to live with love, presence, and emotional mastery. It's a constant reminder that each day is an opportunity to grow, to love, and to make a positive impact on the world around me.

TRENT TAKEAWAYS

- Being direct eliminates unnecessary distractions and draws in excellence.

- God is in control.

- Obstacles are opportunities to test myself.

*"Composure: the art of staying calm, focused,
and resilient in the face of challenges."*

~David Trent

CHAPTER 20

COMPOSURE

ENTREPRENEURIAL INSPIRATION

The Power of Composure:
Navigating Financial Turbulence
with Confidence and Clarity

Throughout my extensive career in wealth management, spanning from 1992 to 2023, I had the privilege to navigate numerous financial storms alongside exceptional clients. As mentioned in the previous chapter, among the most challenging moments were undoubtedly the periods of volatile stock markets, especially during significant financial crises.

The dot-com bubble burst from 2000 to 2002, the Global Financial Crisis from 2007 to 2009, and the unprecedented problems brought about by the COVID-19 pandemic in 2020 are particularly memorable. These crises, each with their unique causes and effects, significantly impacted financial markets, economies, businesses, and individuals worldwide.

However, early on in my journey, I gleaned a vital lesson—volatility in the markets is a recurring event, almost an annual ritual. With each bout of turbulence, my team and I honed our ability to maintain composure. We viewed these problems as opportunities for growth and improvement.

I remember a particularly tense team meeting during the 2008 financial crisis. One of our junior advisors, Sarah, was visibly stressed.

"How can we possibly reassure clients when everything seems to be falling apart?" she asked.

I took a deep breath and replied, "Sarah, remember, we've been through market downturns before. Our job isn't just to manage money, it's to manage emotions. Stay calm, focus on our long-term strategies, and our clients will follow our lead."

If I can instill confidence in my team, they will be able to do the same for our clients.

This approach indeed proved invaluable when dealing with anxious clients.

As mentioned in the last chapter, during the COVID-19 pandemic, I had a call with a long-time client who was on the verge of panic-selling his entire portfolio.

"David, I can't take it anymore," the client said. "The market's crashing, and I feel like I'm losing everything. I think we should sell before it gets worse."

I responded calmly, "I understand your concerns. But remember, we've built your portfolio to withstand these kinds of shocks. Selling now would lock in losses. Let's review your long-term goals and see how we can adjust without making drastic moves."

As I reassured him, I thought: *This is where our preparation and strategy pay off. We need to keep our clients focused on the bigger picture.*

While we weren't infallible, we excelled at keeping our clients calm, preventing them from making impulsive decisions driven by panic that could have had long-lasting consequences.

Maintaining composure proved to be a critical skill, especially during financial and economic upheavals. It significantly influenced how effectively we communicated, consoled, and guided our clients. By staying composed, we approached problems with a clear mind, analyzed situations objectively, evaluated risks, and made strategic decisions to navigate our days with resilience and expertise.

Moreover, composure played a pivotal role in counseling clients facing financial setbacks. Our calm and empathetic demeanor allowed us to actively listen to their concerns and offer practical solutions. This approach not only helped them feel understood but also strengthened the bond between us as their trusted advisor, fostering long-term trust and loyalty.

Mary was deeply worried about her retirement savings during the 2008 crisis.

"David, I'm scared. What if I lose everything I've worked for?" she asked, her voice quivering.

"Mary," I replied gently, "I understand your fears. But let's look at your portfolio together. We've diversified your investments to mitigate risks. This downturn doesn't feel temporary, but I assure you it is, and we have a solid plan in place."

As I spoke, I saw the tension easing from her face. "Thank you, David. I feel a bit more at ease now," she said, her voice softening.

The importance of composure in wealth management during turbulent times cannot be overstated. Effectively communicating with clients and consoling when needed helped guide them toward successful outcomes. Our ability to remain composed not only strengthened client relationships but also reinforced trust, ultimately leading to positive and fruitful outcomes for all parties.

I realize composure is more than just a professional skill; it's a mindset that can transform how we navigate life's challenges.

Staying calm in the storm isn't just about survival. It's about finding opportunities for growth and leading others with confidence and clarity.

FAMILY VALUES

From Defeat to Triumph: The Power of Composure and Sportsmanship in Team Success

After my son Carter's 7th grade year, we took a basketball team of eight boys to compete in a summer tournament in Fort Worth, Texas. With only four teams in the tournament, we played on Friday night and had two games on Saturday. Despite losing one game on Saturday, we managed to win two games. The team that beat us was not only unsportsmanlike but also taunted us throughout the game in a crushing 30-point defeat.

I remember the sting of that loss. As the final buzzer sounded, I looked at the boys' faces, seeing a mix of frustration and disappointment. *How do we turn this around?*

However, this tough loss served as a valuable lesson for us. Following a discussion after the game, I emphasized to the boys the importance of good sportsmanship and maintaining composure even in challenging situations.

"Boys," I said, gathering them around, "remember, there are only two things you can truly control in this game, your effort and your composure. No matter what the other team does or says, stay focused on those two things."

Some of the boys nodded, but I wasn't sure the message had fully sunk in. *We need to show them that we're better than this. Not just in skill but in character.*

We had the chance to face the same team again in the championship game on Sunday. Thanks to a brilliant defensive strategy devised by my friend and co-coach Marlon Haynes and improved play, we secured a two-point victory and claimed the tournament championship.

Our composure, execution of the game plan, and refusal to engage with the taunting from the opposing team were key factors in our success. In a timeout with 20 seconds left in the game, I instructed the boys: "Be gracious winners, shake hands with the other team, and avoid celebrating excessively in front of them."

As I spoke, I saw the determination in their eyes. *They get it. They really understand what this is about.* I was proud.

This satisfying victory highlighted the importance of composure, sportsmanship, and resilience. After informing them of the plan, we headed outside, out of view of the other team. I closed the door and let loose with our celebration. The boys rushed out first; it took me a bit longer to join them. When I finally did, we all went wild with excitement.

"David," Marlon said, grinning from ear to ear, "I can't believe that defensive strategy actually worked!"

I laughed, still catching my breath. "It was all you, Marlon. Your plan was brilliant. These boys executed it perfectly."

I get goosebumps thinking about that moment. The journey from a tough loss to a championship victory taught us valuable lessons about maintaining composure, staying focused on the game plan, and practicing good sportsmanship in all situations. It was a transformative experience that shaped the boys and also me as a coach and father.

As we celebrated, I pulled Carter aside. "Son, I'm so proud of you," I said, my voice filled with emotion. "You showed real character out there."

Carter looked up at me, his eyes shining. "Thanks, Dad. It wasn't easy, but we did it together."

That moment, standing there with my son and the team, I realized something profound. *This isn't just about winning a game—it's about teaching these boys how to handle life's challenges with grace and determination.*

The experience reinforced the importance of composure and sportsmanship, not just in sports, but in all aspects of life. It reminded me that true success isn't just about the outcome, but about how we conduct ourselves along the way.

As I reflect on that tournament, I'm so grateful. Hats off to Marlon; your strategy and support made a big difference.

The lessons we learned on that basketball court continue to resonate—a powerful reminder that with composure, resilience, and a commitment to good sportsmanship, we can overcome any challenge and achieve greatness together.

MASTER TEACHINGS
The Power of Composure: Lessons from John Wooden on Life, Sports, and Character

Composure is a skill that transcends the boundaries of sports, influencing every facet of life. It impacts how we navigate our moments, make decisions, and interact with others. John Wooden, the legendary basketball coach, understood the profound power of composure and its transformative effects on both sports and life.

In sports, composure often serves as the decisive factor between success and failure. Athletes who maintain a calm, focused demeanor and regulate their emotions perform at peak levels. Wooden's coaching philosophy was built on the pillars of poise, discipline, and mental toughness, which significantly contributed to the success of his UCLA team.

I remember watching old footage of Wooden on the sidelines. I admired his calm presence, radiating serenity and assurance. *How does he stay so composed?*

His teams were always impeccably prepared and displayed such composure that Wooden often took a more passive role during games. Rather than resorting to frantic coaching with his players, he instilled the self-discipline and confidence to flawlessly execute his strategies, resulting in unparalleled triumphs on the basketball court.

Wooden once said, "Be quick, but don't hurry." This simple yet profound advice is the essence of composure—acting with urgency but without panic. His calm demeanor and strategic mindset were instrumental in guiding his teams to success.

During a stressful moment in one game I coached, the clock ticked down, and the pressure mounted. Wooden's words helped: *Be quick, but don't hurry*. I took a deep breath, steadied myself, and calmly instructed my team on the next play. The result was a perfectly executed strategy that led to a crucial basket.

Another impactful quote from Wooden is, "Things turn out best for the people who make the best of the way things turn out." This states the importance of maintaining a positive outlook and composure, regardless of circumstances. It taught me to focus on making the best of every situation.

Wooden's words coached me when everything seemed to be going wrong. *How can I make the best of this situation?* By shifting my focus to what I could control and staying composed, I navigated the challenges and found new opportunities for growth.

His emphasis on character over reputation also left a lasting impression. He famously stated, "Be more concerned with your character than your reputation, because your character is what you really are, while your reputation is merely what others think you are." I began to prioritize integrity and authenticity in my interactions, both personally and professionally.

I recall a conversation with a mentee who was worried about how others perceived him. "David, I'm concerned about my reputation," he confided.

"Focus on your character," I replied, echoing Wooden's wisdom. "Your reputation will take care of itself if you stay true to who you are."

Composure extends far beyond the realm of sports. It fosters emotional intelligence, empowering individuals to regulate their emotions, communicate effectively, and make sound decisions even in high-stress environments. John Wooden's iconic Pyramid of Success includes these principles, emphasizing qualities like self-control, poise, and balance as indispensable elements for achieving excellence in life.

Wooden also stated, "Success is peace of mind, which is a direct result of self-satisfaction in knowing you did your best to become the best you are capable of becoming." Embracing composure as a guiding principle equips individuals with the strength and resilience to navigate life's challenges with grace, determination, and steadfast focus. It's a fundamental aspect of personal and professional growth, shaping not just our actions but also our mindset toward achieving greatness.

Wooden's focus on self-improvement, character, and composure became guiding principles in my life. Whether facing financial crises, coaching a basketball team, or navigating personal challenges, his quotes provided a roadmap for maintaining composure and striving for excellence.

Success is peace of mind. Am I doing my best to become the best I am capable of becoming? This introspection led to renewed commitment.

John Wooden's teachings continue to guide me through both ordinary days and extraordinary challenges, reminding me that true success is achieved through calm, focused determination and unwavering integrity. By embracing these principles, I found deeper fulfillment and resilience, shaping my actions and mindset toward achieving greatness.

TRENT TAKEAWAYS

- Poise, discipline, and mental toughness are key components of composure.

- Composure cultivates emotional intelligence.

- CALM–Composed, Assertive, Level-headed, Masterful.

"Adversity introduces a man to himself."

~Albert Einstein

CHAPTER 21

FEAR

ENTREPRENEURIAL INSPIRATION
Embracing Fear: Transforming Challenges into Opportunities for Growth

My determination was put to the test many times. But I never allowed setbacks to shape my identity. Instead, I embraced them as chances to gain knowledge, evolve, and bring innovation into play.

One day, sitting at my desk, after enduring a lot of rejection, I doubted myself.

Is this really worth it? Am I cut out for this?

But then I took a deep breath and reminded myself: *This is part of the journey. Every 'no' gets me closer to a 'yes.'*

Trent Capital Management witnessed a consistent expansion, drawing in a group of ten exceptional team members who shared my enthusiasm for helping families with their financial management. By the year 2020, we were honored to serve more than 200 families and oversee assets surpassing $200 million. This extraordinary accomplishment was proof of our strategic guidance and dedication to our clients' prosperity.

I recall the day we hit the $200 million mark. As I shared the news with my team, I was so proud and grateful. "We did it, team," I said, my voice thick with emotion. "This is just the beginning."

The crises in 2007-2008 and 2020 tested our resilience and adaptability, prompting us to embrace the FEAR acronym: Face Everything and Rise, or Forget Everything and Run. Inspired by the quote from Zig Ziglar and Pitbull's empowering anthem, *I Believe That We Will Win*, this mindset empowered us to confront adversity with courage.

During the 2008 financial crisis, I remember a tense team meeting. One of our advisors was visibly stressed, his voice trembling as he asked, "David, how are we going to get through this?"

Recalling the words from Zig Ziglar, I looked him in the eye and said, "We have two choices: we can face everything and rise or forget everything and run. I choose to rise. Who's with me?"

The room fell silent for a moment, then one by one, my team members nodded in agreement. It was a turning point for us.

In 2021, I merged my company with another well-established entity—a game-changing decision. This bold move not only broadened our horizons but also paved the way for new opportunities and partnerships. By carefully strategizing and looking ahead, I divested a part of my stake in the merged company, laying the groundwork for a gradual departure from the business. Another Face Everything and Rise (FEAR) moment.

I remember feeling excited and apprehensive. *Is this the right move? Can I trust the new partners to uphold the values and standards we built?*

As I signed the merger documents, my hand shook *This is it, no turning back now. But this is how we grow, by facing our fears head-on.*

By early 2023, as our assets under management soared past $1 billion, I made the bittersweet decision to fully exit and sell the remaining portion of my interest to my younger partners in the business I nurtured for almost 27 years. A FEAR moment struck again. This transition marked the culmination of my entire transformative journey filled with invaluable lessons in grit, determination, strategic vision, and the power of resilience in the face of adversity—my legacy.

Walking away from something I built from the ground up was one of the hardest decisions I've ever made. But I knew it was time to embrace new challenges and opportunities.

Shortly after, I came across a photo of our team in 2019 before we merged. Tears welled up in my eyes. *We've come so far. It's time for a new chapter.*

This journey taught me that true entrepreneurial spirit isn't just about building a successful business; it's about having the courage to face your fears, embrace change, and continually evolve. Each FEAR moment became a stepping stone to greater heights, reinforcing the power of resilience and adaptability.

As I embark on my next adventure, I carry all these lessons with me. The FEAR acronym became more than just a motivational tool; it's a way of life. It reminds me that every challenge is an opportunity for growth, and that by facing our fears, we can achieve things we never thought possible.

FAMILY VALUES
Facing Challenges with Grace:
Lessons from a Life of Service and Sacrifice

In the 1920s, circuit rider preachers were the embodiment of dedication and resilience. They traveled through vast rural territories to spread their message. These itinerant ministers played a crucial role in bringing spiritual guidance to isolated communities that lacked established churches. Their lives were characterized by adventure, hardship, and commitment to their faith and mission.

One such preacher was my wife Tiny's grandfather, Giles Pixley. Called to preach in the late 1920s, Giles began his Methodist ministry on foot in north central Arkansas, walking between remote rural areas to deliver his sermons. With little more than a Bible in hand and an unshakeable faith, he traversed rough terrains and winding mountain paths, bringing spiritual nourishment to those in need.

"Lord, give me the strength to reach those who need Your word, no matter the distance or difficulty," Giles often prayed, determined.

Life as a circuit rider preacher was far from glamorous. Giles often faced harsh weather conditions, enduring rain, snow, and scorching heat on his journeys. Nights were spent in modest accommodations, ranging from the homes of parishioners to makeshift shelters in the wilderness. Despite the physical toll of his work, Giles pressed on, driven by a sense of duty and divine calling.

I often wondered how he kept going in the face of such adversity. It was a question that filled me with both admiration and curiosity.

As Giles's ministry grew, so did the support from the communities he served. He eventually acquired a horse, which eased his travels between congregations. Later, in a generous act of kindness, someone gifted him a Model-T car, enabling him to reach even more distant areas. This progression from foot to horse to car showed the growing appreciation and reliance these communities had on their circuit rider preacher.

"Thank You, Lord, for providing me with the means to reach more of Your children. May I continue to serve them faithfully," Giles prayed, his heart filled with gratitude.

In the early days, Giles's income was minimal, often reliant on the meager donations from the impoverished communities he served. He was often paid in food instead of cash. Parishioners offered what they could: potatoes, chickens, and other goods. These tokens of gratitude sustained him physically and also strengthened his bond with the people he served. Giles accepted these humble offerings with grace, understanding that they represented the deep respect and appreciation of his flock.

I remember Tiny sharing proud stories about her grandfather. "He never complained," she said. "He always saw those gifts as blessings, no matter how small."

The isolation of his work posed another significant challenge. Far from his family and home church, Giles relied on his resourcefulness and faith to cope with loneliness. He developed deep relationships with the people he served, becoming not just a spiritual leader but also an integral part of the community fabric. His visits were eagerly anticipated events, providing religious instruction and a sense of connection and continuity for the scattered populations.

"Even in my solitude, I feel Your presence, Lord. Let me be a beacon of Your love and strength to these communities," Giles prayed, finding solace in his faith.

Giles Pixley never let physical, emotional, or financial challenges deter him. He was a true model of the Face Everything and Rise mentality, conquering doubt and opposition with remarkable patience, diplomacy, and determination. Giles passed away at the age of 89, leaving behind a legacy that speaks volumes about the lasting influence of his commitment to sharing his message with the world.

What drove him to keep going?

The answer, I realized, lay in his unwavering faith and his deep love for the people he served.

One evening, I asked Tiny, "What do you think was the most important lesson your grandfather taught you?"

She smiled softly. "He taught me that true strength comes from within, and that no matter how tough things get, you can always find a way to keep going if you have faith."

Giles's story is a powerful reminder that facing hard times with grace and resilience leads to a life of profound impact and fulfillment. His legacy inspires me, reminding me that no matter the obstacle, we can always find the strength to rise above and make a difference in the lives of others.

MASTER TEACHINGS
From Scrolls to Success: Embracing Persistence, Emotional Mastery, and Positivity

As mentioned earlier, Og Mandino's *The Greatest Salesman in the World* provided profound wisdom in its ten scrolls. Four of these enlightening scrolls especially embodied the mindset behind FEAR (Face Everything and Rise).

"I will persist until I succeed" became my mantra and I reminded myself of this during times I was faced with market downturns or challenging client situations.

At one point, I had to fire a team member that was a poor culture fit. As I sat in my office, feeling defeated, Mandino's words helped. "I will persist until I succeed," I whispered to myself. "This is just a temporary setback."

Success often comes, not to the most talented, but to those who refuse to give up. I incorporated this teaching by setting small, achievable goals each day, celebrating minor victories, and using setbacks as learning opportunities.

"Today I will be a master of my emotions" proved invaluable in high-stress situations. In the volatile world of finance, maintaining composure is crucial.

I practiced this in my daily prayer routine and implemented a "pause and reflect" approach before reacting to any crisis. This helped me make more rational decisions and better guide my clients through turbulent times.

"I will laugh at the world" transformed my perspective on challenges. Instead of viewing obstacles as burdens, I began to see opportunities. One day, after a series of setbacks, I caught myself smiling.

Why am I smiling?

I realized I was finally seeing the humor in the situation, just as Mandino taught. I started keeping a victory journal, where I wrote down successes and the lessons learned from failures, often with a humorous twist. This practice helped me maintain a positive outlook during all kinds of moments.

"I will pray for guidance" became a cornerstone of my decision-making process. Before major business moves or during periods of uncertainty, I made it a habit to seek spiritual guidance.

There was a crucial moment when I considered a major business merger. Feeling overwhelmed, I turned to prayer. "Lord," I said, "I need Your wisdom. Guide me in this decision."

This practice provided me with inner peace and clarity, and often led to insights I might have otherwise missed. There's wisdom beyond our immediate understanding.

These teachings, combined with an attitude of facing challenges head-on, shaped my approach to both personal and professional life. They taught me to view FEAR not as something to run from, but as an invitation to rise and grow.

One mentee struggled with fear of failure. "David, how do you handle the fear of making mistakes?"

I smiled, thinking of Mandino's teachings. "I've learned to see fear as an opportunity," I replied. "It's not about avoiding fear, it's about facing it and rising above it."

By incorporating these principles, I was equipped to navigate the complexities of the financial world (and life in general), always striving to face everything and rise.

I'm filled with gratitude for the wisdom Mandino shared. Og, your scrolls have guided me through the storms.

These teachings, as all I've shared, are more than just words on a page; they're a way of life. With persistence, emotional mastery, and a positive outlook, we can overcome any challenge and achieve greatness.

TRENT TAKEAWAYS

- Embrace challenges as opportunities for growth and learning.

- Financial crises can be turning points for innovation and adaptation.

- THRIVE–Transformation, Harmony, Resilience, Innovation, Vision, Empowerment.

"It's not what you look at that matters, it's what you see."

~Henry David Thoreau

CHAPTER 22

PERSPECTIVE

ENTREPRENEURIAL INSPIRATION
Barry Shore and the Impact of Mindset on Entrepreneurial Success

I discovered the transformative power of perspective—a lesson similar to Barry Shore's inspiring story. Barry's life took a dramatic turn when he was paralyzed overnight due to a rare disease. This life-altering event could've crushed his spirit, but instead, Barry chose to see it as an opportunity to redefine his purpose and impact the world in meaningful ways.

Time and again, my perspective on people, events, and situations played a pivotal role in navigating challenges, finding solutions, and achieving success. One of the fundamental keys to my success is understanding that perspective is everything. Instead of being bogged down by what I can't control, I focus relentlessly on what I can do and influence. This shift in perspective empowered me to take proactive steps, make strategic decisions, and steer my journey with purpose.

During another difficult time, I sat in my office, staring at the quarterly reports, feeling the weight of the world on my shoulders. "How am I going to turn this around?" I muttered to myself, frustrated.

A mentor, Tom, happened to call me that afternoon. "David, how's everything going?" he asked, sensing the tension in my voice.

"Honestly, Tom, it's tough. The numbers aren't looking good, and I'm feeling uncertain," I admitted, doubtful.

Tom paused for a moment before responding. "David, remember Barry Shore's story? He didn't let his circumstances define him. He focused on what he could control and found new ways to make an impact. What's one thing you can control right now?"

I took a deep breath. *He's right. What can I control?*

I realized I could control my response to the situation, my attitude, and my actions. I decided to focus on improving our client service and building stronger relationships with our clients.

Barry Shore's colorful approach to life and impactful mindset mirrored my own beliefs. Like Barry, I understood the importance of maintaining a positive outlook no matter what. His use of acronyms like "JOY" (Journey of You) and "SMILE" (Start My Internal Love Engine) resonated. Attitude and perspective are powerful tools for shaping reality.

The practice of focusing on what I could control and taking decisive action in those areas was powerful. This approach boosted my confidence and allowed me to communicate effectively with clients, networks, and friends. Clear communication meant bridging gaps, fostering trust, building meaningful connections, and ultimately, success.

One potential client was hesitant to invest in our services. "David, I'm just not sure if this is the right move for us," he said.

I leaned forward, maintaining eye contact. "I understand your concerns, and I appreciate your honesty. Let's focus on what we can achieve together. Here's how we can address your specific needs and ensure a successful partnership," I replied, outlining a tailored plan. As I spoke, I saw his apprehension start to fade, replaced by a sense of trust and optimism.

In every instance, I embraced Barry Shore's philosophy of finding gratitude, resilience, acceptance, and trust (GRAT), which guided me through uncertainties, setbacks, and moments of doubt, reminding me to stay focused on the bigger picture and the positive impact I could make.

The synergy between Barry Shore's story and my journey underscores the profound impact of perspective. By embracing a colorful, joyful, and impactful mindset, we can turn obstacles into opportunities, setbacks into stepping stones, and challenges into catalysts for growth.

Perspective isn't just a lens through which we view the world; it's a powerful force that shapes our reality, influences our actions, and drives us towards success and fulfillment.

FAMILY VALUES
Tiny Notes, Big Impact:
How Gratitude Shapes Our Journey

My wife Lisa, affectionately known as Tiny, crafted a tradition that embodies the transformative essence of perspective. Over the past decade, on cherished occasions such as anniversaries, Valentine's Day, birthdays, and Christmas, she surprised me with a bag brimming with tiny notes—my beloved strips.

I remember the first time she presented me with one. It was our anniversary, and as I opened it, confusion flickered across my face. "What's this?" I asked, peering into the bag filled with colorful paper strips.

Excited, Tiny said, "Open one!"

I unfolded the first strip, and felt that lump in my throat. Written in neat typewritten text were the words, "Your determination inspires me every day." I looked up, overwhelmed with emotion. "Tiny, this is. . .incredible," I managed to say.

These strips, each carrying a sentiment of love, humor, admiration, or cherished memories, became a treasure trove of positivity and affection. They are gestures of endearment but also profound lessons in perspective.

Each bag contains anywhere between 30 to 50 of these precious strips, making them the most extraordinary gift I could ever dream of. With around forty of these bags in my possession, each filled with an average of 40 notes, I've amassed over 1500 notes in total—showing the depth of love and care Tiny pours into this tradition.

I'm struck by the impact of this gift on my life, both personally and professionally. They've become a profound source of inspiration, motivation, and resilience that has shaped my perspective.

During a bad day of doubting my abilities as a leader, I reached into my desk drawer and pulled out one of Tiny's bags.

Maybe this will help.

The first strip I unfolded read, "Your integrity in business is unmatched." I felt a wave of reassurance. *She's right. I need to trust my instincts and stay true to my values.*

Indirectly, the strips influenced my mindset, infusing each day with positivity, optimism, and gratitude. They are gentle, empowering reminders of the love, support, and belief that surround me.

Sentences like "You care deeply about your team and clients," "You are an inspiration to many young men entrepreneurs," "You continue to learn, explore, and build upon your goals," and "You are a great connector of people," reinforce values, strengths, and aspirations.

During a team meeting, I repeated words from one of Tiny's strips: "You have a gift for bringing out the best in others." I looked around at my colleagues.

How can I apply this to our current project? How can I help each person here shine?

What began as a heartfelt tradition changed my perspective, and guided my decisions, actions, and interactions in both personal and professional realms. The strips remind me of the importance of empathy, integrity, and hard work—values integral to success and fulfillment.

"You know," I said to Tiny one evening, "these strips of yours—they've changed the way I see everything. They're like. . .like a compass for my soul."

She smiled warmly. "That's all I ever wanted them to be," she replied, squeezing my hand.

Tiny's thoughtful gesture, though seemingly small, had a profound impact on my journey. It's a reminder that perspective isn't just about how we view the world; it's about finding joy, gratitude, and purpose in every moment, no matter how small or ordinary it may seem.

As I hold each strip, I'm reminded of the power of perspective and the transformative impact of love and support in shaping our journey.

MASTER TEACHINGS
Embracing Optimism: Transforming Life's Manure into Hidden Blessings

Once upon a time, in a tale woven with contrasts, there lived a pair of identical twins whose outlooks on life couldn't have been more different. One twin was a perpetual optimist, greeting each day with the exuberant proclamation, "Everything's coming up roses!" Meanwhile, the other twin wore the cloak of pessimism, always bracing for the worst.

As I read this story, I paused. *Which twin am I more like?*

Concerned about their children's divergent attitudes, the parents sought the guidance of a wise psychologist. This expert of the human mind proposed an intriguing experiment to help balance their personalities as they approach their upcoming birthday.

"Let's try something unconventional," the psychologist suggested, leaning forward in his chair. "We'll give the pessimistic twin the best toys money can buy and the optimistic twin a box of manure. This will help us understand their reactions and perhaps guide them towards a more balanced outlook."

What an unusual approach! But isn't that how life often works? We don't always get what we expect.

On the auspicious day, the twins were ushered into separate rooms to unveil their gifts. Following the psychologist's counsel, the parents presented the pessimistic twin with the finest toys money could buy, while the optimistic twin received a humble box filled with manure.

Eager to witness their children's reactions, the parents surreptitiously observed from afar. They were disheartened to hear the pessimistic twin grumble about the toy's color, predict its imminent demise, and compare it unfavorably to other grander toys.

"This toy is going to break any minute," the pessimistic twin muttered, shaking his head. "And it's not even the right color. Why couldn't I get something better?"

How often have I focused on the negatives instead of appreciating what I have? I was uncomfortable with the realization.

Their hearts heavy with concern, the parents ventured to the optimistic twin's room. What they beheld left them awe-struck and inspired. The optimistic twin was gleefully tossing the manure into the air, laughter bubbling forth like a mountain spring. With sparkling eyes, he declared, "You can't fool me! Where there's this much manure, there must be a pony!"

The optimistic twin's reaction amused me.

What a beautiful way to look at things, finding hope and opportunity even in the most unexpected places.

Do I approach life like the pessimistic twin, always expecting the worst? Or do I embrace challenges with the optimism of the other twin?

Do we approach each day with trepidation, anticipating mishaps and disappointment? Or do we embrace life's unpredictability with open arms, anticipating blessings in every circumstance?

My outlook and perspective shape my experiences and colors how I interpret the world. I resolved to approach each day with a renewed sense of optimism and curiosity, ready to uncover the hidden ponies in every challenge and embrace the unexpected joys that life has to offer.

The next morning, as I faced a new challenge at work, I caught myself starting to slip into pessimism and I paused.

Where's the pony in this situation?

It was a small shift, but it changed my entire approach to the problem.

How we view our circumstances can profoundly impact our experiences and outcomes. It's not about ignoring difficulties, but about finding the potential for growth and joy even in the most unexpected places. Now, when faced with challenges, I often ask, "Where's the pony?" It's a simple question, but one that has the power to transform.

NOTE: *The story about the optimistic and pessimistic twins receiving different gifts for their birthday and their reactions is a well-known anecdote often used to illustrate the power of perspective and attitude. This story has been widely circulated in various forms and contexts, including motivational speeches, self-help books, and psychological studies. However, it is difficult to pinpoint a single, original source for this story as it appears to be part of the public domain and has been adapted and retold by many authors and speakers over the years.*

TRENT TAKEAWAYS

- Perspective is the paintbrush that colors our world.

- Positivity Overcomes Challenges.

- VIEW: Value Insightful Understandings, Embrace Wisdom.

"Tough times never last but tough people do"

~Robert Schuller

CHAPTER 23

TOUGH

ENTREPRENEURIAL INSPIRATION

Fighting Spirit: How Legends Inspire Us to Overcome Challenges

Growing up, my love for boxing knew no bounds. It was more than just a sport to me; it became my driving force and a wellspring of inspiration during the toughest moments of my journey. I still remember the first time I watched a boxing match with my father. The energy, the intensity, the raw emotion—it all captivated me.

"Dad, how do they keep going when they're getting hit so hard?" I asked, my eyes glued to the screen.

My father smiled, "That's the heart of a champion, son. They never give up, no matter how tough it gets."

Those words stuck with me years later as I faced my own battles in the business world.

Whether I grappled with initial entrepreneurial financial hurdles, braving the Y2K panic, enduring the tempest of the economic downturn, persevering through the hardships inflicted by COVID, or facing personal trials, I consistently discovered solace and resilience in the defining moments of Muhammad Ali's legendary bout and the inaugural *Rocky* film, which I streamed on YouTube.

During one particularly arduous period, when my business struggled, I remember thinking, *Man, this is so hard; it's brutal. How can I get through this?* I rewatched these iconic matches. As I sat there, my mind raced with doubts and fears. *If Ali and Rocky could keep fighting against such overwhelming odds, why can't I?*

Ali's most unforgettable fight occurred in October 1974, famously known as the Rumble in the Jungle, where he went head-to-head with George Foreman in Zaire. Ali's strategic rope-a-dope technique during that match was truly remarkable. He cleverly let Foreman (who had an impressive 40-0 record) tire himself out by continuously attacking Ali's body while leaning against the ropes for eight rounds. And just when Foreman was completely drained, Ali seized the opportunity to strike back and secure victory.

I remember thinking: *That's it! Sometimes, success isn't about constantly attacking. It's about enduring, adapting, and waiting for the right moment to make your move.*

Similarly, I drew inspiration from a scene in the original *Rocky* movie. Despite being the underdog, Rocky refused to back down even when faced with a relentless beating from Apollo Creed in the ring. Knocked down time and time again, Rocky's unwavering determination was truly awe-inspiring.

When a new, large client proposal deal I worked on for months fell through, I felt utterly defeated. But then I remembered Rocky's words: "It ain't about how hard you hit. It's about how hard you can get hit and keep moving forward."

Come on, David. You've been knocked down, but you're not out. Get up and keep fighting.

In the 14th round, as Apollo unleashed a relentless barrage of punches, it seemed like Rocky was about to be defeated, possibly even knocked out. However, against all odds, Rocky found the inner strength to rise once more, leaving Apollo utterly stunned. The sheer disbelief etched on Apollo's face conveyed a powerful message of Rocky's indomitable spirit.

I could almost hear Rocky's trainer, Mickey, shouting in my ear, "You're gonna eat lightnin' and you're gonna crap thunder!" It made me laugh, but it also gave me the push I needed to keep going.

Watching these two legendary boxing moments fueled my determination to tackle struggles directly, mirroring the resilience shown by Ali and Rocky. I mastered the skill of overcoming difficulties and coming out even stronger, prepared to handle any obstacles that came my way with unwavering assurance and poise, especially when interacting with and supporting clients.

In times when a tough portfolio management decision came up or I faced a difficult client, I thought: *Channel your inner Ali. Stay cool, stay strategic. Your moment will come.* And more often than not, it did.

In business, as in the ring, it's not about avoiding hits; it's about learning how to take them and keep moving forward. Their stories became my personal mantra, reminding me that every setback is just setting the stage for a comeback.

FAMILY VALUES
Lessons from the Breakfast Table: How Courage and Determination Shape Our Journey

My mother's morning ritual of reading the Bible to us over breakfast was more than just a routine; it was a profound lesson. These moments remind me of the timeless tale of David and Goliath, a story that deeply resonated with my mother and mirrored her strength and determination.

I can still hear her voice, clear and steady, as she began each morning: "Let's open our hearts and minds to the Word of God." Her words pulled me from my sleepy state, and I found myself fully alert, eager to hear what wisdom she shared that day.

The imagery of her reading from that massive Bible, resting on a stand at the table, remains etched in my memory. It was as if the sheer size of the book mirrored her affection for the epic tale of David facing the giant Goliath.

"Mom," I once asked, my spoon hovering over my cereal bowl, "why do you like the David and Goliath story so much?"

She smiled. "Because, it reminds us that with faith and courage, we can overcome anything no matter how big or scary it might seem."

In 1 Samuel 17, the formidable Goliath taunted Saul and his soldiers for an astonishing 40 days, challenging them to send a warrior to face him. Despite the fear and hesitation among Saul's men, David, armed only with a sling and stones, stepped forward to confront the giant.

As my mother read this part, I remember thinking, *Wow, David must have been so scared. How did he find the courage?* It was a question that resurfaced many times in my life when I faced trials.

The story of David and Goliath symbolizes courage, faith, and the triumph of the underdog. David's unwavering determination and belief in divine guidance propelled him to face Goliath head-on. With a single, well-aimed shot, David defeated the giant, showcasing the power of resilience, faith, and the willingness to confront seemingly insurmountable ordeals.

"You see," my mother would say, her voice filled with conviction, "David didn't see himself as small or weak. He saw himself as capable because he had faith in God's strength, not just his own."

This story has a deep spiritual meaning—a reminder of God's presence in our lives and the strength we can draw from faith. David's declaration, "I have the Lord on my side," shows the belief in divine protection and assistance, reinforcing the idea that with faith and determination, we can overcome even the most daunting obstacles.

There were moments I felt overwhelmed, facing tough times that seemed as insurmountable as Goliath. In those moments, I heard my mother's voice: "Remember David, You're never alone in your battles."

My mother's ritual of sharing this story every morning instilled in me a sense of tenacity and faith that guided me through life's battles. Just as David faced Goliath with unwavering courage, my mother's teachings instilled in me the belief that with determination, faith, and the support of a higher power, we can conquer our own giants and achieve victory in our endeavors.

Years later, I tried to decide whether to spend a significant sum on new software for my business. I sat at my kitchen table eating breakfast, thinking about those Bible readings. I closed my eyes and whispered, "Mom, I could use some of that David courage right now." And somehow, I felt stronger, ready to face my own Goliath.

These morning lessons weren't just about religion; they were about life, facing fears, and believing in oneself. My mother's wisdom, shared over cereal and orange juice, became the foundation of my resilience and the source of my strength.

Now that my mother is no longer with us, reflecting on these cherished memories has become even more powerful. Her legacy lives on in the lessons she imparted, and I draw strength from her teachings more than ever. Her wisdom continues to guide me. I'm grateful for the enduring power of my mother's love and the timeless nature of her lessons.

MASTER TEACHINGS
Transforming Challenges into Opportunities:
The Power of Mindset

The quote "If God puts a Goliath in front of you, that's because he knows there's a David inside of you" aligns with the teachings of Tony Robbins, a Jim Rohn mentee and renowned life coach and motivational speaker. Robbins' philosophy emphasizes the idea that problems, no matter how daunting, are opportunities for growth and transformation.

I remember the first time I heard Robbins speak. His energy was infectious. I sat there, absorbing his message. *Is this what I've been missing all along? The power to reframe my problems?*

In Robbins' view, every obstacle or "Goliath" that we encounter in life serves a purpose. These tough times are not meant to overwhelm us but rather to reveal our inner strength, tenacity, and potential, just like the story of David and Goliath from the Bible.

"Your problems are not your problem," Robbins' voice boomed. "Your response to your problems is your problem. Or should I say, your opportunity!" I nodded, thinking back to all the times I felt defeated.

What if I had seen them as opportunities instead?

When faced with adversity, Robbins teaches that we should embrace it as a chance to tap into our untapped potential and discover the "David" within us. We too can confront our battles head-on and find innovative solutions to overcome them.

"Ask yourself," Robbins challenged me, "what if this hurdle is here not to stop me, but to make me stronger? What if this is my moment to shine?"

These words lasted long after the seminar. I started to look at my business struggles differently. Instead of seeing them as insurmountable obstacles, I viewed them as opportunities to innovate and grow.

Robbins often speaks about the power of mindset and belief in shaping our reality. According to his teachings, when we adopt a mindset of determination, faith, and confidence in our abilities, we can conquer anything. Instead of viewing obstacles as barriers, we should see them as pathways to personal growth and success.

"Your beliefs become your thoughts, your thoughts become your words, your words become your actions, your actions become your habits, your habits become your values, your values become your destiny," Robbins' words rang in my ears.

"Success leaves clues," Robbins often says. "Find someone who has achieved what you want to achieve and model their behavior. That's your shortcut to success." This advice led me to seek out mentors in my industry, to learn from their experiences and strategies. It was a game-changer for my business approach.

By embracing adversity as an opportunity for growth and unleashing the potential within us, we can transform adversity into pathways toward a more fulfilling and purposeful life.

TRENT TAKEAWAYS

- Fortitude is revealed through experience.

- The path to success is to take Massive, Determined Action.

- God is my Father and Friend.

"Confidence is not 'They will like me.'
Confidence is 'I'll be fine if they don't.'"

~Unknown

CHAPTER 24

CONFIDENCE

ENTREPRENEURIAL INSPIRATION
The Power of Confidence:
Attracting Clients Who Align with Your Values

Our client testimonials at Trent Capital Management truly showcased our dedication to excellence. Let's delve deeper into one specific quality—confidence.

Before establishing TCM, I was aware of possessing a unique blend of two key skills: strong analytical abilities and exceptional people skills. I often thought: *How can I leverage these strengths to create something truly valuable?* The answer came to me during a late-night brainstorming session.

What if I could combine my analytical mind with my ability to connect with people? That could be the foundation of a wealth management service that's truly different.

I was confident I could harness these qualities to provide a top-notch wealth management service that would justify every penny invested by my clients. When I meet with a client or potential client, my confidence in my capabilities is unwavering.

In one meeting with a high-net-worth individual who seemed skeptical about our services, I explained our approach and felt my confidence grow. "Mr. Johnson," I said, "I understand your concerns. But let me assure you, our team's expertise and dedication to your financial goals are unparalleled. We're not just here to manage your money; we're here to help you achieve your dreams."

I was certain I could draw in a potential client for my firm if they were the right fit.

Confidence, as defined by the Webster dictionary, is "a feeling or belief that someone or something is good or has the ability to succeed at something." This is vastly different from cockiness, which is characterized as "someone who is very arrogant and assumes they know all the answers."

I've always been (and continue to be) extremely confident in my abilities, and over time, I assembled a remarkable team around me. It became evident to me that prospective clients discerned a confident entrepreneur when it was clear I (the entrepreneur) did not rely on their money.

It's not about chasing every dollar. It's about finding the right partnerships that will lead to mutual success. While financial gain was undoubtedly a goal, it was essential for me to partner with exceptional clients, not just anyone with money.

Admittedly, I wasn't flawless in this pursuit. However, this awareness enabled me to identify when a client wasn't the right fit. For instance, there was a client who emailed us almost daily and never seemed satisfied.

"Another email from Mr. Smith," my assistant sighed one morning. "He's asking for a complete portfolio review... again."

I felt a knot in my stomach. "This isn't sustainable," I thought. "We're spending more time managing his anxiety than managing his wealth."

We engaged and tolerated this client's constant need for attention for a while, but eventually made the tough decision to "fire the client." It was a challenging choice because the client was not a bad person, just not the right long-term fit for us.

The conversation was difficult. "Mr. Smith," I began, "I've given this a lot of thought. I believe that for your peace of mind and our ability to serve our clients effectively, it might be best if we part ways."

This situation occurred only a few times over 25 years, and I take pride in that.

Having confidence without arrogance was the key to attracting amazing clients. It also gave me the strength to let go of clients who drained our energy and weren't the right fit. I often reminded myself, "It's not about the quantity of clients, but the quality of relationships we build."

FAMILY VALUES
Inspiration Through Example:
Learning Confidence and Humility from Family

Throughout my life, I've been fortunate to have several incredible role models and mentors who taught me the importance of confidence without arrogance. However, there is one person who stands out above the rest—my older brother Keith. His influence on me has been nothing short of extraordinary, and I consider him to be one of the greatest blessings in my life.

From as far back as I can remember, I've looked up to Keith with awe and admiration. He is three and a half years older. To my young eyes, he seemed larger than life. Watching him excel in everything he did filled me with a sense of wonder and aspiration. I wanted to be just like him, follow in his footsteps, and achieve even a fraction of what he accomplished. I knew If I were able to live up to even a portion of his example, I'd be incredibly successful. Keith's achievements and the way he carried himself were a powerful beacon for me, guiding me through my own journey with the hope that I could one day emulate his remarkable blend of confidence and humility.

When I discuss Keith with friends for the first time, I always begin, "He was a super-achiever." Watching him excel just three grades ahead of me in school was truly inspiring. Not only was he the valedictorian of his class of over 400 students in high school, but he was also the student body president. On top of that, he shone in football as a feisty 170-pound offensive tackle, earning the prestigious All-State title. His talents weren't limited to the field, as he was also a standout member of the high school debate team.

I remember one particular evening when I struggled with my homework. Keith walked by my room and noticed my frustration. "Need some help, little brother?" he asked, his voice always calm and reassuring.

"Yeah, I'm stuck on this math problem," I admitted, feeling a bit embarrassed.

Keith sat down next to me and patiently explained the concept. "You see, it's all about breaking it down into smaller steps," he said.

How does he make everything seem so easy?

What set him apart was his ability to exude confidence without a hint of arrogance. This quality made him a delight to watch as a debater and endeared him to everyone. He even delivered a sermon at our church while still in high school—something truly impactful.

Keith went on to pursue electrical engineering at SMU, where he graduated with an impressive 3.9 GPA in just three and a half years. After working as a petroleum engineer for a couple of years, he decided to further his education and attended law school at the University of Texas. Unsurprisingly, he graduated at the top of his section. He then embarked on a successful career as a defense lawyer before eventually becoming the VP of General Counsel at Duke Energy. After he became a finalist for the opportunity to become the CEO of the company and didn't get the position, he chose to retire at the age of 56. Nowadays, he's retired while serving as a board member for three distinct energy companies and making a difference in the world of philanthropy.

Keith had an immeasurable impact on me. Particularly during my formative years, I aspired to be just like him. Striving to reach his high standards pushed me to become the best version of myself. I recall one conversation when I was considering starting my own business.

"Keith, I'm not sure if I have what it takes to start my own firm," I confessed one evening over dinner.

He looked at me with that familiar, confident smile. "David, you've got everything you need. Just remember, it's not about knowing all the answers. It's about having the confidence to find them."

Even to this day, Keith continues to inspire me with his unwavering confidence and remarkable humility. He truly is the epitome of supreme self-assurance without a trace of arrogance.

I often think: *What would Keith do in this situation?* His guidance and example have been a constant source of strength and motivation.

MASTER TEACHINGS
Embracing Confident Humility: The Key to Authentic Leadership and Growth

Norman Vincent Peale's book *The Power of Positive Thinking* inspired me in my 20s and 30s. My mind swirled with self-doubt about my fledgling career when I found it. As I read, I felt a spark of hope ignited.

Peale, a pioneer in the realm of positive thinking and self-improvement, taught a profound lesson about the balance between confidence and humility. One particular passage struck me: "Believe in yourself! Have faith in your abilities! Without a humble but reasonable confidence in your own powers, you cannot be successful or happy."

I pondered these words late into the night. *Is it possible to be both confident and humble? How can I strike that balance in my own life?*

Central to Peale's teachings was the concept of confident humility. He emphasized a strong sense of self-worth and belief in one's abilities, characteristics that underpin genuine confidence. However, Peale cautioned against the pitfalls of arrogance, which he viewed as a hindrance to personal growth and harmonious relationships.

I let arrogance get the better of me very early in my career. After closing a significant deal, I boasted to my colleagues, only to see their enthusiasm dampen. Later, I reflected on Peale's words: "The trouble with most of us is that we would rather be ruined by praise than saved by criticism."

Arrogance often stems from insecurity and a need to prove oneself, whereas true confidence arises from inner strength and authenticity.

Confident humility, as Peale elucidated, involves acknowledging and embracing one's strengths and achievements without resorting to boastfulness or diminishing others. It entails humble confidence, where individuals appreciate their successes with grace and gratitude while remaining open to feedback, continuous growth, and collaborative endeavors.

I struggled with this concept during a philanthropy board meeting. I was confident in my ideas but hesitant to speak up, fearing I might come across as arrogant. Then, Peale's words inspired me: "The way to become really effective is to be yourself, be natural, be sincere."

I shared my thoughts while also actively seeking input from my fellow board members. The result was a more collaborative and successful project.

Peale believed genuine leaders exemplify confident humility by inspiring and uplifting others through their actions, words, and genuine care for others' well-being. He often said: "The more you lose yourself in something bigger than yourself, the more energy you will have."

This perspective transformed and guided my approach to leadership, self-assessment, and interpersonal relationships. I focused on empowering my team rather than seeking personal accolades and cultivated a mindset of confident humility, striving to acknowledge my strengths while being open to learning, criticism, and collaboration.

There were times when I faltered, of course. Some moments challenged my confidence, and I felt it waning. In those moments, I returned to Peale's book and found solace in his words: "Change your thoughts and you change your world."

I then reframed my perspective and approached challenges with renewed confidence and humility.

This balanced approach contributed to my growth and development and fostered positive and enriching interactions. I'm grateful for the wisdom Peale shared, which continues to guide me in striking that delicate balance between confidence and humility.

TRENT TAKEAWAYS

- Stay open to Feedback and Continuous Improvement.

- Own your Strengths with Humility.

- What can you do to treat everyone with kindness and empathy?

"Family is not an important thing, it's everything."

~Michael J. Fox

CHAPTER 25

FAMILY

ENTREPRENEURIAL INSPIRATION

Avery's Journey: Embracing Individual
Passions for Self-Discovery

At my daughter Avery's eighth-grade graduation, she was voted the funniest kid in her class—a delightful surprise for our family. I remember turning to her brother Carter and saying, "Did you know she was the class clown?" We both laughed, realizing how much of Avery's personality we were still discovering. This moment was just one of many that highlighted her unique character and growing entrepreneurial spirit.

As her father, I hoped she shared my passion for basketball. I developed coaching frameworks for her older brother, Carter, and thought, *why not apply the same to Avery?* Despite my enthusiasm, Avery didn't particularly enjoy basketball. One evening, I sat her down and said, "Avery, how about giving basketball one more shot this season?" She agreed, more out of love than interest.

Avery was reasonably talented, but as soon as the season ended, she humorously declared, "Dad, I'm done with basketball." I chuckled, recognizing her determination to follow her own path. Her athletic journey didn't stop there. She was also skilled in soccer, playing for several years before deciding it wasn't her sport either. I remember pondering, *what will capture her heart?*

The turning point came in the seventh grade when Avery discovered volleyball on her own and fell in love with it. She later confessed, "Dad, I just don't like running that much, and volleyball is perfect for me." Her honesty was refreshing, and I admired her self-awareness. Avery played alongside her friends Paige, Sammie, Celeste, and Alissa, from seventh grade through high school, on their school and travel teams. Her talent shone through, earning all-conference status in her junior and senior years, and her high school team reached the state semifinals and finals during those years.

Just as with sports, I offered guidance on her college academic path. "If you're unsure about your major, why not consider accounting?" I suggested. Avery excelled in all her subjects, but after taking an introductory accounting class at Southern Methodist University, she realized it wasn't for her. This reminded me of my earlier request for her to give basketball another try. Instead, Avery chose to major in marketing, a decision that served her well. She secured a job with Oracle in Austin, Texas, after graduation and worked there for four years.

During this time, Avery expressed interest in pursuing an MBA. "Dad, I think I want to go back to school," she told me one day. After applying to several schools, she received a full scholarship for a two-year MBA program in marketing at the Kelley School of Business at Indiana University. It tickled me when she emailed me the letter she received detailing the full ride. She told me excitedly, "They even pay for my health insurance while I'm a student." I got a chuckle out of that—proud Dad moment for me. Avery moved to Bloomington, completed her degree with honors, and is now two years into her career as an Associate Brand Manager for Conagra.

Avery's entrepreneurial spirit began to blossom alongside her professional achievements. She started her own company, Tablestiles, as a side hustle, selling products in her Etsy Shop. Her entrepreneurial journey took an exciting turn when she discovered Susabella (through a business broker), an established company selling products through Etsy and Amazon, with an asking price just under two million.

I remember the phone call vividly. "Dad, I've found this company I want to buy," she said, her voice brimming with excitement. Despite the challenges of acquiring such a business, Avery dove into learning about SBA loans, crafting a growth plan, and pitching the owner on an owner-finance option. Although the acquisition didn't materialize, I was incredibly proud of her determination and the knowledge she gained through the process. As a side note, the owner of Susabella, who founded the company from scratch 20 years earlier, reached out to Avery. "I see so much of myself in you," she told her, which made me incredibly proud. Avery's determination and passion resonated with the owner, who genuinely wanted Avery to succeed in acquiring the business.

I watched Avery navigate this terrain and turn over every rock, just like I did in my early entrepreneurial days. Her efforts to understand the complexities of business transactions and her desire to grow her entrepreneurial skills are commendable. I'm excited about the future and confident her entrepreneurial spirit will continue to flourish.

Avery's adventurous nature and zest for life remind me of my mother, Donnie Lou, who was all about fun and family. It's heartwarming to see that same spirit of exploration alive in Avery. She has already traveled internationally more than I have in my lifetime, and her close bond with her sister-in-law, Mercedes, is a blessing. Mercedes, an only child, is married to my son Carter, and the friendship between her and Avery is something I cherish deeply. Avery also enjoys card games and board games, a pastime that brings our family and friends together and showcases her playful side.

Reflecting on Avery's journey, I'm grateful for the lessons she learned and the path she's forging. Avery's entrepreneurial spirit is a source of inspiration, and I'm eager to see where her journey will lead her next.

FAMILY VALUES
A Legacy of Love and Faith

Growing up in the Trent family, the bonds we shared were as rich and layered as the antiques my sister Terry and our mother, Donnie Lou, adored. Terry, the eldest of us siblings, was eight years my senior and shared a particularly deep friendship with Mom. Their love for antiques was more than a hobby; it was a shared passion that took them to antique auctions in different cities and even led them to share a booth at a local antique mall. What was it about those old treasures that brought them so close? Perhaps it was the stories each piece held, much like the stories woven into our family fabric.

Terry's connection with Mom was evident from the start. She was eight when I was born and was hoping for a sister, given she already had a brother, Keith. When I arrived with my carrot-colored hair, her initial disappointment was palpable. "I wanted a sister!" she exclaimed, her hands on her hips, though I think she quickly warmed up to me. I must have grown on her, as we became close. Eight years later, when little brother Steve arrived, Terry had come to terms with being surrounded by brothers and she admits today, "I adored my new baby brother."

As we all grew older, married, and had children, the first five grandchildren were boys. It wasn't until I was 31 that my daughter Avery was born, finally breaking the streak. I remember the joy in Terry's eyes, and Mom's too, as they welcomed a little girl into the family. "Finally, a princess!" Terry declared, beaming with pride. *It took 31 years, but it was worth the wait*, I thought, seeing their delight.

Terry's devotion to family was unwavering, especially after Mom passed away at 72. She stepped in to support Dad, filling the void left by Mom's absence. Mom and Dad's 54-year journey together was a testament to partnership and love. Despite battling several health issues, including three types of cancer, Dad remained upbeat, always encouraging others. "How's it going," he was always quick to ask, his spirit unbroken. Terry's presence was a comfort, and her role as a caregiver showed her patience and kindness.

Her oldest son, RJ, shared a special bond with Dad, whom he affectionately called Tapaw. As the first grandchild, RJ had the privilege of naming him. They spent countless times together, watching sports, going out to eat on Saturday nights, or simply enjoying each other's company. I often marveled at the ease with which they communicated, a silent understanding that needed no words. Occasionally, they shared a cigar, a ritual that seemed to seal their bond. RJ's infectious personality and his talent for engaging others with thoughtful questions never fails to light up our family gatherings.

Terry and her husband, Robert, raised their children, RJ and Ryan, with deep-rooted faith, a commitment evident in their long-standing membership at Calvary Baptist Church. They joined two years into their marriage and remain dedicated members to this day. Their faith was the cornerstone of their family life, a guiding light through both joyous and tough times. Terry's home became the heart of family gatherings, whether for holidays, birthdays, or any celebration. "You all know you're always welcome here," she always insists, her arms open wide.

Her love for the lake, particularly visiting our brothers' lake houses in South Carolina and Texas, was another testament to her love for family. "Nothing beats a great family gathering at the lake," she would say, her voice filled with nostalgia as we reminisced about our times together.

I delivered the eulogy at Mom's funeral, highlighting her fire and faith—traits Terry embodies to this day. Fiercely loyal and caring, she carries on Mom's legacy, nurturing our extended family with the same warmth and dedication. Standing at the podium, I felt the weight of Mom's legacy on my shoulders, a legacy Terry carried with grace and strength.

Terry and Robert's journey began at Arkansas State University, where they met and fell in love. After graduation, Robert pursued a career in pharmacy at Baptist Hospital, while Terry embarked on a career where she served in many roles at Entergy. Remarkably, both stayed with their first employers for over four decades—Robert for 42 years and Terry for 43. Their steadfastness mirrored their commitment to each other and their faith, much like their enduring membership at Calvary Baptist. Their love story was one of dedication and mutual respect, modeling the values instilled in us by our parents. They're just as much in love today as when they first got married and still really enjoy spending time together. Just like Mom and Dad, loving and supporting their family is very important to them. They now have two precious grandchildren who bring much joy to their lives.

Reflecting on her relationship with Mom, Terry once shared, "Mom was a phenomenal influence and example growing up, and as adults, we were the best of friends. We loved to shop together and cherished our time at the antique booth. I could tell her anything; she was an awesome mother and best friend." Listening to Terry, I realized how much mom's spirit lived on in her. I'm grateful for the legacy of love and faith that shaped our family.

As I look back, I see how these values have woven a beautiful fabric in our lives, guiding us through obstacles and celebrating our joys. What would I do without the support of my family, knowing that the love we shared was our greatest treasure?

MASTER TEACHINGS
The Power of Family Values in Shaping Generations

As I reflect on the concept of master teachers in life, my thoughts immediately turn to my younger brother Steve (53) and his wife Katy (52) Trent. Their journey in raising an exceptional family while Steve navigated the challenges of entrepreneurship has become a beacon of inspiration for our entire extended family.

Steve's path as a serial entrepreneur has been remarkable. I remember when he started his first company, Drive Financial, with partners, and the excitement in his voice as he told me, "Davey," as he calls me, "this is it! This is how I'm going to create the life I want for my family," was palpable. That venture was just the beginning. He later launched Southern Transportation, which he successfully sold after 16 years while continuing to work for the parent company, now Triumph Insurance.

What struck me most was how Steve leveraged his entrepreneurial success to be an exceptional father and husband. "Entrepreneurship isn't just about building businesses," he once told me. "It's about building the life you want." This philosophy allowed him the flexibility to be present for his family in ways many couldn't.

After he sold Southern Transportation, he reflected, "You know, Davey, the ups and downs of building a business have taught me more about resilience and leadership than any book ever could. And I get to pass those lessons on to my kids."

Steve and Katy's four children—Josie (22), Evie (20), Baker (18), and Rush (15)—have grown up in an environment where faith, family, and the entrepreneurial spirit are seamlessly intertwined. I've often wondered how they balance it all so gracefully.

One summer evening at their lake house near Mount Vernon, Texas, I watched as Steve gathered the family for prayer before dinner. "Lord," he began, his voice steady and warm, "we thank you for this time together, for the tough stuff that makes us stronger, and for the love that binds us." The respect in his children's eyes was evident. It was a powerful moment. This is what a strong family looks like.

Their lake house has become more than just a vacation spot; it's a crucible where their family bond has been forged. I recall Katy saying, "Our best memories are made here, away from the distractions of everyday life." This intentional focus on family time resonates with John Maxwell's teaching that "strong families don't just happen. They take time, commitment, and a willingness to grow together."

We often joked about Steve being an "uh-oh" baby, conceived during an insurance convention in St. Louis. "St. Louis Steve," we called him, much to his amusement. "You know," Steve chuckled, "being the youngest has its perks, like having all of you as my role models."

The impact of Steve and Katy's approach to family life extends beyond their immediate circle. They've become unofficial master teachers for our entire clan. I was particularly moved when my nephew Wilson, Keith's son, confided in his cousin Carter about his aspirations for his own young family.

"You know, Carter," Wilson said, his voice filled with admiration, "Martha and I really want to raise our kids the way Uncle Steve and Aunt Katy did. There's just something special about how they've balanced success and family." He paused, reflecting on his own experiences. "I think part of it is because we were teenagers when they started their family. Watching them as parents taught us so much."

This conversation sparked a mix of emotions in me. On the one hand, I felt immense pride in Steve and Katy's influence. On the other, I realized that Wilson wasn't dismissing the valuable lessons from his own parents, Keith and Lucy. Instead, he was seeking to blend the best of both worlds—

the strong foundation laid by his parents and the inspiring example set by Steve and Katy.

Interestingly, Carter and his wife Mercedes also admire Steve and Katy for the way they raised their family. Although Carter and Mercedes don't have children yet, I'm sure when they do, they'll use Steve and Katy as models. It's comforting to know that the values we cherish are being passed down to future generations.

As I watch the next generation of our family begin to form their own households, I'm filled with a sense of gratitude and hope. The legacy of strong family values, coupled with the entrepreneurial spirit exemplified so beautifully by Steve and Katy, continues to shape our family tree.

I had a conversation with Steve not long ago. "You know, Davey," he said thoughtfully, "raising a family while building a business isn't about being perfect. It's about being present and intentional, and using every experience—good or bad—as a teaching moment." Those words stuck with me, challenging me to continually reassess and improve my own approach to family life and business.

In the end, the greatest lesson I've learned from observing Steve and Katy is that a truly strong family nurtures its own members and inspires others. Their example reminds me of Maxwell's wisdom: "The greatest legacy one can pass on to one's children and grandchildren is not money or material things, but rather a legacy of character and faith."

The master teachings of Steve and Katy, built on the foundation laid by our parents and enriched by the lessons of entrepreneurship, have created a beautiful mixture of family life that continues to evolve and inspire.

TRENT TAKEAWAYS

- Intentional family time strengthens bonds.

- Integrate entrepreneurial spirit with family life.

- Encourage family to pursue their unique interests.

IN CLOSING AND ENCOURAGEMENT

As we reach the culmination of *Elevate Others: Lessons for Purpose-Driven Entrepreneurs*, I invite you to reflect on the transformative power of lifting others as you pursue your own path to success. Throughout this book, we've explored how the true essence of authentic business success lies in our ability to elevate those around us. This principle has been the cornerstone of my journey, from the early days of founding Trent Capital Management to the heights of breaking the billion-dollar barrier in assets under management.

In the vast landscape of entrepreneurship, where dreams meet challenges and ambitions carve intricate paths, one truth remains clear: when we prioritize the well-being of others, we unlock the potential within ourselves. This is the heart of purpose-driven entrepreneurship—it's about building a community of support, inspiration, and shared success.

As you move forward, I encourage you to embrace this philosophy in every aspect of your life. Seek opportunities to uplift those around you, whether in business, family, or personal growth. Share your knowledge, offer your support, and celebrate the successes of others as if they were your own. By doing so, you create a ripple effect that extends far beyond yourself, enriching both your life and the lives of those you touch.

Remember, elevating others is not just an act of kindness; it's a strategic approach to achieving lasting success and fulfillment. When we help others rise, we elevate ourselves in the process.

So, as you close this book, I challenge you to take action. Identify someone in your life who could benefit from your encouragement or guidance. Reach out, offer your support, and witness the profound impact that simple acts can have.

Thank you for joining me on this journey. Together, let's commit to elevating others and, in doing so, elevate ourselves and the world around us. Embrace the journey and let the spirit of altruistic egoism guide you to new heights.

ABOUT THE AUTHOR

From a young age, David Trent was captivated by the world of entrepreneurship, fascinated by the potential to transform ideas into successful businesses. This passion initiated a journey that has spanned decades, marked by continuous learning, growth, and achievement.

David's entrepreneurial path began with the founding of three companies, two of which he built from the ground up. Among these ventures, Trent Capital Management stands out as a testament to strategic vision and perseverance.

Starting at the age of 33, David nurtured this firm into a formidable entity, and by the time he exited at 60, it managed over a billion in assets. A guiding principle for him is, "Success is not just about what you achieve, but about the impact you make on others along the way."

Currently, David focuses on empowering leaders through his role as Chairman of multiple CEO Peer Groups with LXCouncil. These groups create a confidential and collaborative environment where CEOs can share insights, tackle challenges, and drive growth. He believes that "The best ideas often come from the conversations we have with one another," emphasizing that collective wisdom fuels innovation and success.

Driven by a desire to share experiences and insights, David authored "Elevate Others: Lessons for Purpose-Driven Entrepreneurs." This book reflects his belief that true success lies in empowering others and fostering a culture of collaboration and growth. As he often reminds readers, "When we lift others, we elevate ourselves."

As the Founder and CEO of Trent Premier Growth, David is dedicated to helping businesses and leaders realize their potential. His team, one of the few in North America composed of Pinnacle Business Guides and Certified Exit Planning Advisors (CEPAs), offers tailored solutions to meet each client's unique challenges and goals.

Additionally, as an M&A advisor with Optima M&A, David leverages his extensive experience to guide businesses through complex mergers and acquisitions. At Optima, the focus is on an old-fashioned approach built on timeless values such as trust, integrity, and personal service.

Whether for aspiring entrepreneurs or seasoned executives, David is committed to supporting their journeys. Together, they can transform visions into reality and create a lasting impact.

Trent Premier Growth: https://trentpremiergrowth.com/

LinkedIn: https://www.linkedin.com/in/david-trent-82612016/

Contact David to inquire about speaking at your event by contacting him by email at: david@trentpg.com

Our legacy is defined not just by what we achieve,
but by how we elevate others along the way.

~ David Trent

Made in the USA
Columbia, SC
05 May 2025

57455717R00122